Twice-Exceptional Children *Are* Gifts

The exceptional is all around us. Our job is to recognize that every child, in fact, every person, has gifts to contribute to our world.

John Inman

Twice-Exceptional Children *Are* Gifts
Developing the Talents of 2e Children

John Inman

Learning Exceptionalities Press
Tacoma, WA

First published 2020

by Learning Exceptionalities Press
Tacoma, WA

© John Inman

All rights reserved. No part of this book may be reprinted or reproduced or utilized in any form or by any electronic, mechanical, or other means, now known or hereafter invented, including photocopying and recording, or in any information storage retrieval system, without permission in writing from the publisher.

Trademark notice: Product or corporate names may be trademarks or registered trademarks and are used only for identification and explanation without intent to infringe.

Library of Congress Control Number: 2020912201

ISBN 978-1-7353333-1-1 (pbk)
ISBN 978-1-7353333-2-8 (hbk)
ISBN 978-1-7353333-0-4 (ebk)

Typeset in Palatino linotype
by Monotype Typography, Inc

Section quotes drawn from whitebison.org

Cover illustration by Michael Huayu An, instagram.com/michaelanart

Portrait by David Inman Photography, https://davidinmanphotography.com/

Book design by John Inman

Printed and bound by IngramSpark.

Dedicated

To 2e children everywhere, may your gifts be recognized, developed, and nurtured

To my wife

My son, and

My daughter

Table of Contents

Acknowledgments xv

Authors Note on Approach to Research   xvii

   This Book is an Autoethnography   xvii

   Epistemology – Knowing and Learning About Social Reality   xxiv

   Theoretical Perspective of the World   xxvi

   Themes in This Book   xxvii

   Anticipated Outcomes   xxix

PART ONE

The World of Twice-Exceptionality and a Path Toward Healing

   Chapter 1: My Journey   3

   Chapter 2: Definitions of Gifted, Learning-Disabled, and Twice-Exceptional Learners   7

   Twice-Exceptional   7

   Learning Deficits   10

   Giftedness   12

   Chapter 3: Indigenizing Mainstream Education   15

Chapter 4: Why This Research and a Plea for Change   21

    Who Are These Children?   21

    Creating a Sense of Urgency to Address This Gap   24

    Hope for the Future   28

PART TWO

My Journey, An Autoethnography

Chapter 5: A Brief Autobiographical Sketch   33

Chapter 6: Early Reading Problems   37

    My K-5 Experience   37

Chapter 7: Middle School Years: Another 5th Grade and Private School   49

Chapter 8: High School   61

Chapter 9: My Undergraduate College Years   69

Chapter 10: The Journey to My First Master's Degree   75

    The Impact of Living as a 2e Person   75

    Why I Chose to Earn a Master's in Adult Education   75

    Consulting Coming to an End   81

Chapter 11: Overcoming Barriers to Dialogue   85

    Internal Barriers to Dialogue   86

    External Barriers to Dialogue   91

Chapter 12: A Call to Action   97

PART THREE

A Deep Dive into Theory and Practice: What Does the Literature Say

- Chapter 13: Foundation in Literature   103
- Chapter 14: Twice-Exceptional Learning   105
  - Significant Literature   107
- Chapter 15: Indigenous Foundations for Education   123
  - Look to The Mountain   125
  - Teaching Truly   128
  - Summary of Literature   131

PART FOUR

Indigenous Learning and the Theories Supporting It

- Chapter 16: Indigenous World View of Education   135
  - A Holistic View of the Learner and Their Environment   136
  - Indigenous Foundation for Learning   140

PART FIVE

Insights, Conclusions, and Recommendations

- Chapter 17: Insights and Conclusions   165
- Chapter 18: Future Research Directions and Applications   173

Appendix A: Proposed Classroom for 2e Children 177

Appendix B: Mind Map of Foundational Resources 179

Bibliography 181

Index 193

About the Author 199

Table of Figures

Figure A.1 Framing autoethnography as a "Native" method of inquiry.   xx

Figure 2.1 Gifted, LD, and GLD patterns with John Inman pattern overlaid.   9

Figure 2.2 John Inman IQ chart with subdomains.   10

Figure 4.1 Comparison of Indigenous vs. Western living Four Arrows & Narvaez, 2014.   25

Figure 6.1 Lytton School in Palo Alto, CA where John Inman experienced his first six years of school.   38

Figure 6.2 Second-grade class at Lytton School, Palo Alto, CA.   40

Figure 6.3 Grandparents farm in Mansfield, Arkansas.   41

Figure 6.4 John Inman on the farm in Mansfield, Arkansas.   42

Figure 6.5 John Inman note home 8/20/1960.   43

Figure 7.1 Ford Country Day School, Los Altos Hills, CA.   50

Figure 7.2 Eighth-grade graduating class at FCDS (John Inman upper left).   53

Figure 7.3 Plantation Camp, CA where John Inman spent three summers.   57

Figure 7.4 John Inman (middle right) at Plantation Camp.   58

Figure 8.1 Nishimachi school, Tokyo Japan ninth-grade class (John Inman on left).   62

Figure 8.2 My father, Louis Howard Inman, in the field for SRI.   67

Figure 9.1 John Inman with an Airedale Terrier puppy, his favorite breed.   71

Figure 10.1 John Inman at the radio station in Portland, OR.   78

Figure 10.2 John Inman and Larry Wilson at Pecos River Learning in New Mexico.   80

Figure 11.1 Dialogue then deliberation model Inman, J., & Thompson, T. A. (2013).   93

Figure 14.1 Alphabet children Baum and Owen (2004).   110

Figure 15.1 Dimensions of Indigenous education model, John Inman   126

Figure 16.1 Education is a process of following tracks/multiple pathways, John Inman.   144

Figure 17.1 Circle of courage, Brendtro & Larson, 2004.   171

Acknowledgments

Thank you so much, Katrina Rogers, for believing in me, even when I was demanding, hard to guide, and falling off track. Without your caring and guidance, this journey would never have happened. Four Arrows, you have been a wonderful mentor and guide. You had a vision of what I could do well before I did and made sure I realized my potential. There were many times I was lost and bewildered and it would take but a moment for you to help me see the path. Thank you, my friend. Rodney Beaulieu, I do not think I would have ever selected an autoethnography as my method without your passion and guidance. And even when I chose this path, I still had no idea what it was. Thank you for your patience as I learned to use this amazing approach. Dina Brulles, you helped me open my eyes and embrace gifted education, a field so foreign to me it was not even on my radar. Thank you for your guidance and passion for 2e and cluster grouping education. Roan Kaufman, you stepped in at the last moment and provided excellent insights. Thank you for being willing to join my journey.

A special thank you to Barnett Pearce who reached out of retirement to provide love, support, and friendship. God rest your soul, Barnett. And maybe the most important contribution Barnett made was to bring my cohort together in scholarship to explore CMM—Romi Boucher, Bart Buechner, Sergej van Middendorp, and John Baugus. All have become friends and this journey would have been far more difficult without their guidance, support, and friendship.

Thank you to Diane Montgomery for your willingness to provide a detailed analysis of my pre-doctoral learning assessment and your review and recommendations for the book manuscript. Your kindness and professional input helped me develop the confidence to do this work and publish this book.

Thank you to Brent Warner, Ford Country Day School, who took me as a fifth-grade dyslexic student and helped turn my life around and to Don Prickel, Oregon State University Graduate School of Education, who accepted me into his master's degree cohort when the university felt I was unable to do graduate work. Both have been important guides and mentors on my journey.

Thank you to my parents, Louis Howard Inman and Geraldine Louise Inman, both deceased, who refused to believe my early elementary educators' claims that I was slow and lazy (before dyslexia was recognized in education) but knew otherwise and made substantial sacrifices to help me when others did not believe in me. I would not have completed my dissertation and this book without the foundation they provided for me. Thank you, Mom and Dad.

Thank you to my ex-wife, Hazel, who was the most loving and supportive partner imaginable. Without her support and belief in me, this journey would not have been possible. My children have loved and supported me throughout my journey and have made many sacrifices along the way. My son and my daughter, both outstanding scholars, have been extraordinarily supportive. I am blessed to have a wonderful family.

Author's Note on Approach to Research

My essential research question for this autoethnography, was, *In what ways might an Indigenous worldview have changed how I experienced life as a twice-exceptional learner?* In this book, I tell my story, I address social justice concerns, and reach out to your lived experiences as a reader. You may focus only on my story or you may dive deeply into the theories underpinning this book. Each section can stand on its own depending on what you would like to explore. The basic format of the book flows from this note to you on how and why I approached this topic the way I did, an introduction and background that provides the context for my story, my autoethnographic story, and then sections on twice-exceptional and Indigenous research and a deep dive into Indigenous learning theory. I end with insights and conclusions. I hope you enjoy what I have presented and welcome a conversation about how this work can be used to heal and to develop the gifts every student brings to their education.

This Book is an Autoethnography

Although I address why I chose autoethnography woven throughout the conversation on methodology, a deeper reason for the choice of autoethnography motivated my decision. I chose autoethnography because of its power for change and its impact on the greatest number of people possible. Most people outside of the academy do not find research papers based on quantitative or qualitative research an accessible format. I find quantitative and qualitative research often dry, data-driven, and expert-based, an approach less accessible to nonacademics. An autoethnography can be more accessible as it supports a story format, a casual voice, and it allows me to reach out and engage you, the reader, in my experience. Autoethnography also honors the role of stories and myth in learning, a critical aspect of my work. We learn and transform from stories. My story is designed to transform mindsets. Since I want to create social change, the more people who can access this work, the better chance I have in fulfilling my mission. As well, I cannot be silenced by researchers or practitioners coming from specific biases as they have no data or opinion countering my experience. With an autoethnographic approach, I have a voice and can contribute not only to my healing but to the healing of others who grow up with similar experiences.

An autoethnography written by a researcher looking at his experience analytically does not just tell a story (Ellis, Adams, & Bochner, 2010). As an autoethnographer, I have research literature, tools, and methodologies to help me explore epiphanies from my lived experience in such a way that others might realize they have had similar epiphanies. My epiphanies specifically emerge from my experience growing up as a 2e learner in the Western educational system. Rather than comparing or contrasting my experience with existing research, I compared my experience with an envisioned experience of introducing traditional Indigenous learning principles into my learning environment. I also used existing research to help inform both the experience of living as a 2e individual and learning in an Indigenous learning environment. Not only do I intend to help both insiders and outsiders to education understand the cultural experiences 2e children share, but I also designed this work to address the social injustice experienced by 2e children in learning environments where unmet educational needs lead to failure to realize their potential. I recommend how to overcome this social injustice through the introduction of Indigenous learning foundations into Western education.

My autoethnographic writing is partnered with "Indigenous autoethnography" (Whitinui, 2013). Although I am not Indigenous, respecting, and integrating principles from this method of inquiry helps keep my writing authentic and focused on the social justice ramifications of my lived experience in a greater cultural context. Whitinui explains:

> Indigenous autoethnography as a resistance-discourse is intended to inspire people to take action toward a legitimate way of self-determining one's collective and cultural potential. Indigenous autoethnography also aims to "construct" stories that invoke a deep sense of appreciation for multiple realities and lives concerning indigenous peoples' ways of knowing. (p. 481)

Indigenous autoethnography goes beyond constructing stories, it specifically focuses on resistance of the dominant histories taught in school by first deconstructing Western historical accounts then reconstructing those historical accounts with Indigenous histories (Whitinui, 2013). Four Arrows (2013) specifically asks educators to deconstruct then reconstruct historical accounts when he proposes Indigenizing Western education. I cannot write about Indigenizing Western education without first embracing an Indigenous method of inquiry.

Four key attributes of Indigenous autoethnography emerge from Whitinui's (2013) research. All four key attributes helped me develop my story. The four key attributes include:

- **Ability to "protect"** one's uniqueness. This implies that writing about our own "storied" lives moves beyond simply "validating" knowledge to one of "celebrating" who we are.
- **Ability to "problem-solve"** enables an indigenous person to consider making several 'adjustments' that help to craft a story that is well-reasoned, trustworthy, and authentic.

- **Ability to "provide"** greater 'access' to a wide range of different methods, scenarios, experiences that not only support our social, cultural, and spiritual well-being...., but also supports the wider indigenous collective...

- **Ability to "heal"** is achieved when "learning" about "self" is seen to be critical to one's existence and survival as a collective of cultural human beings (pp. 478-479).

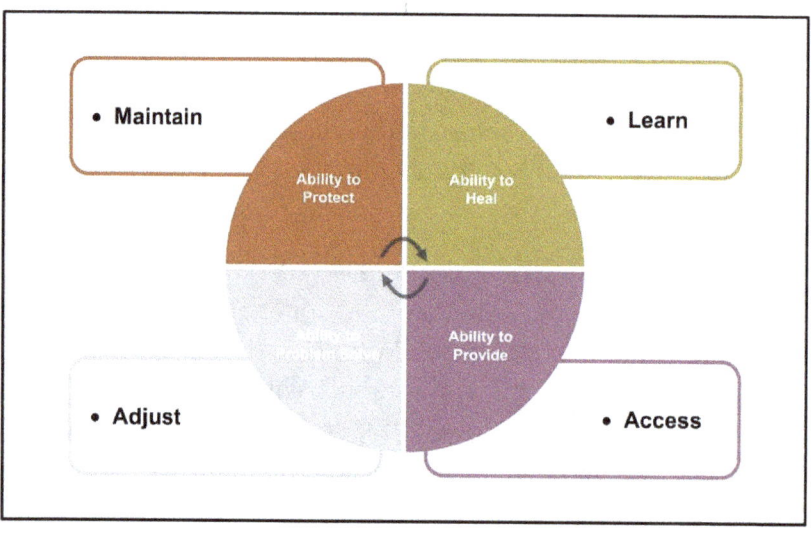

Figure A.1 Framing autoethnography as a "Native" method of inquiry.[1]

At its core, Indigenous autoethnography is about healing one's self and healing of the other. Ricoeur (2010) explains, "for it is only when we translate our own wounds into our own language of strangers and retranslate the wounds of strangers into our own language that healing and reconciliation can take place" (p. xx). Embracing the healing aspect of Indigenous autoethnography has helped me keep the other firmly a part of this work.

---

[1] Used with permission of Sage Publications Inc. Journals, from Indigenous autoethnography: Exploring, engaging, and experiencing "self" as a Native method of inquiry, Whitinui, P, 43(4), 2013; permission conveyed through Copyright Clearance Center, Inc.

I see the biographical focus of autoethnography as important because my story and my experience provide the foundation for the book. Having my experience situated in the greater social context lets me provide social commentary about the lack of social justice for 2e children in the current system. Providing what my experience might have been like in a more just environment, in this case by adding envisioned Indigenous learning foundations to current learning environments, allows me to challenge the system to change and provide a more socially just framework for educating 2e children.

As a researcher, I clearly define how I use the term autoethnography, so I do not confuse researchers and readers. The term autoethnography as a research method has been used somewhat loosely, which has generated confusion and critics (Chang, 2007). Complex combinations of ethnographic research processes, culture, and self, provide the foundation for autoethnography. The complexity arises due to each researcher having more or less emphasis on each of the three facets of the methodology. A right combination does not exist, but Chang cautions, "Whichever style autoethnographers decide to employ, autoethnographers are advised not to lose the sight of the quintessential identity of autoethnography as a cultural study of self and others" (p. 11). Although difficult, I kept the focus on culture and self at the front of my mind as I constructed my research. I found it much easier to focus on self than the ethnographic research process and the cultural connection of my story.

Although I started writing in preparation for the autoethnography 9 years ago, I did not realize my writing had prepared me for ethnographic research. I persistently kept returning to this path as if guided here. My need to eliminate the pain for other children that I experienced growing up 2e provides a possible explanation for the root of my persistence. My past writing had been autobiographical and based on my memory of my experiences.

However, difficulties arise when relying on memory alone as memories often prove unreliable.

Chang (2007) suggests helping autoethnographers remember events in stories through data derived from field texts collected using five strategies. The first strategy recommends using visual tools. Although I have extensive pictures of my life as I grew up 2e, I used only a few pictures to help visualize my experience. The second strategy suggests inventorying people, artifacts, mentors, values, experiences, and activities. I used this strategy extensively in my writing. The third strategy involves chronicling my history and life cycle. I wrote in this format from an autobiographical perspective highlighting those experiences most meaningful to my journey as a 2e learner. The fourth strategy includes reading and responding to other autoethnographies. I did not use this strategy. The fifth strategy recommends collecting artifacts of many types. I had not considered this strategy but found some school records and writings from my grade school and middle school years useful. These artifacts provided more background and support for my story.

Chang (2007) outlines three styles of autoethnographic research. An autoethnographer must understand each and choose which to use. The three styles include realist, confessional, and impressionist styles. The realist captures in detail the experience, the confessional focuses on the personal experience, and the impressionist focuses on the experience of the fieldwork itself. My research uses the confessional style of autoethnography. Chang also outlines three benefits of writing an autoethnography. The first benefit suggests both the researcher and reader find the method friendly, the second benefit includes both self and others gaining cultural understanding, and the third benefit outlines the potential of cross-cultural coalition building for both self and others. As the subject of an autoethnography, the researcher has a holistic and intimate perspective, an advantage unavailable in other research methodologies.

Autoethnography as a researcher friendly methodology helped me write and tell my story. When writing the autoethnography, I used my voice which made my story more interesting to write and hopefully more interesting to read than with other narrative styles. Gergen and Gergen (2002) explain, "In using oneself as an ethnographic exemplar, the researcher is freed from the traditional conventions of writing. One's unique voicing – complete with colloquialisms, reverberations from multiple relationships, and emotional expressiveness – is honored" (p. 14). Self-examination and self-reflection have been advantages for me during my research journey. Just a few months before starting my doctoral dissertation, I did not even know 2e existed let alone accepted my giftedness. I had lived a lifetime thinking I grew up broken and in need of fixing. My self-reflection made this journey worthwhile even if I derived no other benefits. Through the process of self-reflection, I come to understand "forces" making me similar to, different from, or in opposition to others. Finding others who have had similar experiences has been transformative, the third benefit of an autoethnography.

Educators are beginning to embrace the emerging field of study of understanding how to develop healthy learning-disabled and gifted children. Rather than seek insights from experts in the field of either gifted or learning-disabled education to tell me about the experience, reflecting on my own experience of growing up 2e felt more authentic. My story and my experience of the world through my story have had a profound impact on my life.

As a child growing up 2e, I like other 2e children met grade-level standards and educators ignored me, or if they helped, they placed me in remedial programs. I grew up believing I had no gifts, the same belief many other 2e children experience. I see social justice issues as educators funnel 2e children into remedial programs where they often feel inferior.

Indigenous learning foundations first interested me during the new student orientation for my doctoral program at Fielding Graduate University. In a conversation with another student who grew up with similar experiences, we imagined what it would have been like to grow up in an Indigenous environment where we would have been honored for the gifts we brought to the community rather than considered broken and in need of fixing. My need to tell my story of growing up 2e, my desire to create a socially just educational system for all children, and my interest in Indigenous learning provide the foundation for why I chose autoethnography as my methodology.

I have coupled my autoethnography with literature research of applicable Indigenous worldviews. I positioned the Indigenous worldviews to explore how my lived experience might have been different within an Indigenous context.

Epistemology – Knowing and Learning About Social Reality

Indigenous teaching and learning perspectives especially in the Americas, have a strong matriarchal aspect. Therefore, feminist epistemology provides the fertile soil from which my story emerges (Lessem & Schieffer, 2008; Luke & Gore, 1992). A feminist epistemology provides the context to fully express other epistemologies in the book. These other epistemologies include constructionist epistemology (Ackermann, 2001; Gergen & Gergen, 2004; Harel & Papert, 1991; Pearce, 2009a), which provides an exploratory and subjective framework for my autoethnography; process epistemology (Hernes, 2008, 2010; Hernes & Maitlis, 2010), which provides an understanding that entities, as found in rational paradigms, give way to everything being in a state of becoming; borderlands epistemology (Harding, 1996), which provides an understanding for the liminal aspects of transformational learning; and indigenous epistemology (Battiste, 2008) as the dialogic core of my autoethnography and as the spiritual center of this book. I consider myself a constructionist theorist, and feminist epistemology as a constructionist framework forms the foundation for my practice and the methodology in this book. Harel and Papert (1991) explain:

> Traditional epistemology gives a privileged position to knowledge that is abstract, impersonal, and detached from the knower, and treats other forms of knowledge as inferior. But feminist scholars have argued that many women prefer working with more personal, less detached knowledge and do so very successfully. If this is true, they should prefer the more concrete forms of knowledge favored by constructionism to the propositional forms of knowledge favored by instructionism. (p. 10)

A further conversation about feminist epistemology provides an understanding as to why I think embracing a framework born from women's experiences can be authentic for me. The foundation for this fit comes from my belief that the illusion of objectivity and the power differential found in many types of research between the researcher and the researched must be reduced for real social change addressing inequities in our system to emerge. Sprague (2005) says, "Many feminists reject the mainstream ideal of a disengaged, 'value-free' science, arguing instead that the goal of research must be to understand how oppression works and to provide knowledge that will help fight against injustice" (p. 8). This thought underlying feminist epistemology directly supports indigenous, constructionist, and borderlands epistemologies and my theoretical perspective.

I implemented a feminist epistemology by focusing on my socially embedded experience shared with others and rejected my position as the expert researching subjects. Using dialogic approaches to creating relationships and the co-creation of new knowledge and perspectives at the borderlands (knowledge is socially constructed), continues to be my approach to reducing social injustice. A feminist epistemology also provides an alternative to a positivist epistemology based on objectivism which forms the foundation for the mechanistic and dualistic Western approach to education and learning, an approach particularly damaging to me growing up as a 2e learner. My systemic worldview and a feminist epistemology embrace system thinking assuming a deep connection between all aspects of a system and rejecting narrow objective answers to systemic problems. Using a feminist epistemology helped guide my exploration of my experience growing up and living as a 2e learner and has focused my efforts on eliminating the social injustice I experienced for others who like me, struggle with mechanistic and dualistic learning environments. Maxine Green explains, "Feminist pedagogies . . . demand critical examination of what lies below the surface. They demand confrontations with discontinuities, particularities, and the narratives that embody actual life stories" (Luke & Gore, 1992, p. x). In this way, a feminist epistemology directly supports my autoethnographic approach to my research with a focus on relationships, dialogue, co-creation of new knowledge, systems, and social justice.

Theoretical Perspective of the World

I view all things in the world as connected and given this view; I believe analyzing the parts does not inform one of the whole. Viewing all things as connected generates a whole systems worldview, a worldview supported by Indigenous thought (Four Arrows, 2013; Cajete, 1994). During my evolution as a systems thinker, my theoretical interest in systems has been further refined to a focus on human systems. A human system does not conform to a hierarchical system but a system as patterns of communication with a foundation in dialogue. The human systems view informs my story and supports my worldview. My systems framework has a paradox. As a human, I exist as a living system and a part of the world as a complex system, Gaia. At the same time as a human, I exist as part of a human social system, a system based on communication process, not a living system framework.

Themes in This Book

I provide a deep dive into the theories, models, and research woven throughout the book in parts three and four. So that references in parts one and two have context, I will review the basic models here even though they are covered in more depth later.

Cluster grouping (Brulles & Brown, 2018; Winebrenner & Brulles, 2008) provides a recommended framework for how to organize the learning space for twice-exceptional and other children and is referenced throughout the book. The basic concept of cluster grouping is to keep children in the classroom with their friends and peers while providing appropriate instruction to their learning capabilities. Cluster grouping prevents children from feeling different and like "the other." Groups of similar students are grouped together with three or four groups per classroom. Not all classrooms will be cluster-grouped and only teachers who have a talent and passion for teaching a cluster-grouped classroom will be assigned to these classrooms. The added benefit to a school and school district is that separate classrooms do not need to be set up and staffed for each level of learning.

The Indigenous educational processes that are explored in this book are drawn from *Look to the Mountain* (Cajete, 1994). There are an array of theorists and epistemologies provided in parts three and four that contribute to and validate the principles outlined in *Look to the Mountain*. Throughout the exploration of Indigenous principles, these theorists and epistemologies are drawn on to provide support for the elements of Indigenous education. A mind map of these foundational resources is found in Appendix B. There are also several Indigenous themes woven into the development of this educational paradigm. The first theme is concentric circles. Concentric circles form a consistent model for much of American

Indian thought. The second is the theme of the hunter of good heart. The hunter of good heart is someone that is on a journey to become whole.

Three other themes are woven into this book. The first is a "sense of place" (That place that Indians talk about). Critical to Indigenous education is a sense of place, a bonding to the home, the village, the region, and the mountain. Place is central to understanding who we are and what our place is in this world and can be developed by Indigenous and non-Indigenous people alike regardless of the setting, be it urban or rural. Jeannette Armstrong, in her essay "Keepers of the Earth," explains this (Armstrong, 1995):

> As Okanagans, our most essential responsibility is to learn to bond our whole individual selves and our communal selves to the land . . . . We join with the larger self, outward to the land, and rejoice in all that we are. We are this one part of the Earth. Without this self we are not human: we yearn; we are incomplete; we are wild, needing to learn our place as land pieces. We cannot find joy because we need place in this sense to nurture and protect our family/community/self. The thing Okanagans fear worst of all is to be removed from the land that is their life and their spirit (p. 323).

The next theme is a "connection with and respect for all persons, human and non-human." In Indigenous mythology all persons are to be respected and protected whether they are alive or not. This is not a Western philosophy of stewardship over as an ecological concept but understanding that all persons are related, are family (all persons, human and non-human). This Indigenous ecology is one of love and respect of family. And lastly but connected to ecology is 'spiritual ecology', a deep understanding that all that we do starts and ends with spirit. The spiritual is not something outside of us, it is not the worship of an entity, but provides purpose for everything we do. Whether making tools, art, or learning, it is for the community not for self-indulgence (Cajete, 1994).

Anticipated Outcomes

I have begun to understand myself and how I relate to and experience the world through my in-depth reflection of my lived experience of being 2e and exploring the work of others who study and write about this emerging field. As I reflect on Indigenous learning foundations and how they might have provided a healthier experience growing up 2e, I hope my reflections and lived story provide hope and inspiration to others who struggle in the Western educational mindset within which educators ask us to learn and grow. If my story can spark a conversation and contribute to this important emerging field of study, I have fulfilled my mission.

John Inman

Part One
The World of Twice-Exceptionality and a Path Toward Healing

"But the great spirit has provided you and me with an opportunity for study in nature's university, the forests, the rivers, the mountains, and the animals which include us."
-- -- *Walking Buffalo, STONEY*

Chapter 1
My Journey

The steps in my doctoral journey profoundly transformed me as a learner and researcher. The journey built on a lifelong foundation of dialogue. The consistency of this theme did not reveal itself until 2 years into my doctoral journey. Growing up as a twice-exceptional (2e) child taught me to survive early in life through my ability to listen and synthesize all the disparate inputs swirling around me. Twice-exceptionality, also known as dual exceptionality or gifted and learning-disabled (LD) (Gifted and LD or GLD), describes the patterns I and other 2e children experience. I learned differently than others, saw the world differently, and thought differently. The pattern of communicating, thinking, and hard work learned early has framed my development and provided the foundation for my work.

My worldview results directly from growing up as a 2e child. While others saw and memorized discrete entities, the Creator blessed me by seeing connections and patterns. From my earliest memories, I saw the world as a whole, not as separate and disconnected. A holistic worldview helps me embrace complexity, uncertainty, and ambiguity rather than one-dimensional patterns and solutions. This gift informs my view on topics as diverse as human relations where people co-create their relationships to environmental challenges where simple statements of solution ignore the complexity of what we have created. In many respects, my worldview corresponds more closely to a holistic and connected Indigenous worldview than a dualistic and mechanistic Western worldview.

Unfortunately, my perspectives were not supported or even recognized by the educational system based on a Western worldview. Had an Indigenous worldview foundation for teaching and learning existed, my growing up 2e might have been significantly different.

I came to this work understanding the importance of different ways of knowing and believing many others with different ways of knowing must experience something like my experiences. Through an autoethnographic approach to my doctoral dissertation and this book, I envisioned having a positive impact on how children of all ways of knowing can develop and contribute to the world. My experience as a 2e learner, combined with my interest in how my experience might have been different if my learning environment had been infused with Indigenous learning principles, creates my particular interest in writing an autoethnography and my hope of informing k-12 educators through a conversation on how to improve learning for 2e children: In actuality all children. This quest brought me to the doctoral program at Fielding Graduate University to do the work captured in my dissertation. I have translated that work into this book. My research question for my doctorate in education was, *In what ways might an Indigenous worldview have changed how I experienced life as a twice-exceptional learner?*

As an Anglo-European, I sense the importance of the historical context of Indigenous people in a dominant Anglo-European culture. My sensitivity to Indigenous peoples came early in life from my father's interest in Native Americans and their ways of life. I was raised to not only respect Indigenous peoples but to embrace Indigenous principles and their importance to me as I was growing up. With this said, I do understand the possible sensitivity to me writing about an Indigenous topic with no experience of the content or context of Indigenous history or culture. Given this sensitivity, I will clarify my motivations in my use of traditional Indigenous principles (Indigenous throughout the rest of the book). I apply my interest in Indigenous principles narrowly. The Indigenous experience has many social and historical issues, but my specific interest and the only interest I qualify to address involves how to use Indigenous learning principles to improve current k-12 education for 2e and other alternative learning children. I have no interest in being anyone other than myself. I have no romantic illusions about what it might have been like to live hundreds of years ago in an Indigenous setting. I draw from Indigenous principles as a student and learner on a journey to develop into a whole human being and continuously gain personal insights and understanding from the exploration of 2e education and my life as a 2e learner. The whole human being journey derives from "the hunter of good heart" (Cajete, 1994), an ancient metaphor for the quest for "completeness reached through an educational process involving the hunter's whole being" (p. 59). My discovery journey revealed through my autoethnography will hopefully inform how I can contribute to the world and bring a sense of peace within myself.

Wisdom not only exists in Western thought and history, but wisdom also exists in ancient Asian, South Asian, African, Pacific, Middle Eastern, and American Indigenous practices and philosophies. I eagerly learn from traditions with a focus on application to create a better and more just world. I approach Indigenous learning foundations from this mindset. For this book, when I refer to *Indigenous,* I am referring to American Indigenous, which includes Indigenous peoples from Alaska to the southern tip of South America. The definition of Indigenous I use means peoples sharing historical traditions, culture, spirituality, language, and place who inhabited the Americas before colonization. I have chosen to focus on American Indigenous peoples given their spiritual connection with the land in the Americas and the probability my topic might resonate with those readers who live in the region.

Chapter 2
Definitions of Gifted, Learning-Disabled, and Twice-Exceptional Learners

By the very nature of twice-exceptional or gifted and learning-disabled (GLD), a child has gifts in some domains and deficits in others. To understand the nuances of learning as a 2e child, we need working definitions of twice-exceptional, giftedness, and specific learning disorders as 2e children need an educational setting designed to address multiple exceptionalities. Although many in the field use disabled or disorder to label a child with a learning deficit as stated above, positive psychology would challenge this notion. When I use common terminologies based on the underlying literature such as *disabled* or *disorder*, I am referring to a deficit. Demonstrating a disability or disorder in a domain does not constitute a pathology, it is simply a deficit (Brendtro & Larson, 2004). As gifts and deficits are genetic traits, humans display a full range of gifts and deficits as normal variability in the population.

Twice-Exceptional

According to Baum (2012), education leaders established the Joint Commission of Twice-Exceptional Education to address a pervasive and ongoing unwillingness on the part of educators to accept children who simultaneously demonstrate both gifted and learning-disabled tendencies. Not only has educator reluctance to recognize 2e resulted in the continued under-identification of 2e children, but 2e children also rarely receive the services they need to thrive. The commission acted early on to establish a working definition of twice-exceptionality and the needs of twice-exceptional learners.

Baum presents this working definition and it serves as a guide to my work:

> Twice-exceptional learners are students who have evidence of the potential for high achievement capability in areas such as specific academics; general intellectual ability; creativity; leadership; and/or visual, spatial, or performing arts AND also have evidence of one or more disabilities as defined by federal or state eligibility criteria such as specific learning disabilities; speech and language disorders; emotional/behavioral disorders; physical disabilities; autism spectrum; or other health impairments, such as ADHD.
>
> Identification of twice-exceptional students requires comprehensive assessment in both the areas of giftedness and disability, as one does not preclude the other. Educational services must address both the high achievement potential as well as the deficits of this population of students.
>
> Twice-exceptional students require differentiated instruction, accommodations and/or modifications, direct services, specialized instruction, acceleration options, and opportunities for talent development. Twice-exceptional students require an individual education plan (IEP) or a 504 accommodation plan, complete with goals and strategies that enable them to achieve growth at a level commensurate with their abilities, develop their gifts and talents, and learn compensation skills and strategies to address their disabilities. This comprehensive education plan must include talent development goals. (p. 1)

Often educators fail to grasp the implications of living as a 2e child and the above definition helps frame an understanding. To help understand the differences, the graph in Figure 2.1 (Nielsen, 2002) provides a picture of IQ and performance differences in gifted, 2e, and LD children. I have added my pattern to put my 2e

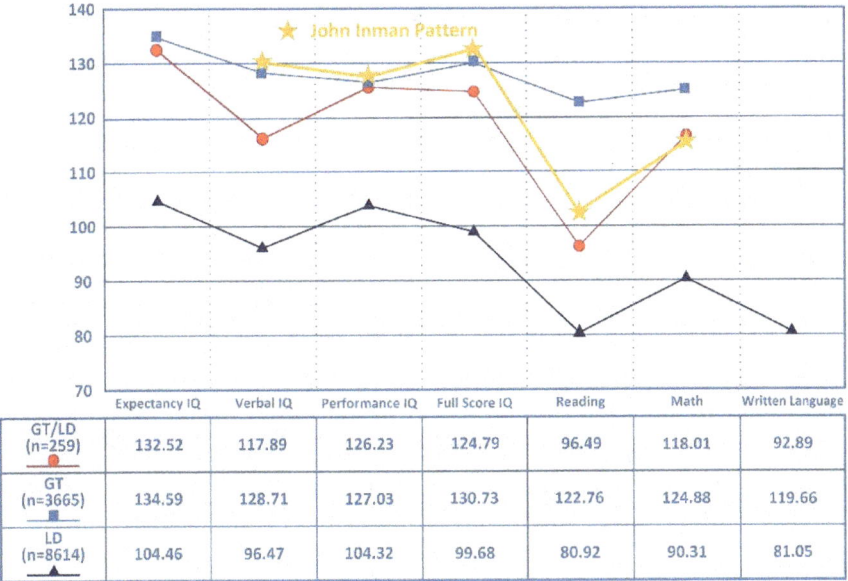

Figure 2.1 Gifted, LD, and GLD patterns with John Inman pattern overlaid.[2]

experience in context. Giftedness and learning disability are domain-specific. Figure 2.2 on the following page provides examples from my pre-doctoral evaluation with the Wechsler Adult Intelligence Scale – Third Edition and the Woodcock-Johnson III Test of Achievement in 2009. These results have helped me understand my experience and introduced me to the field of 2e learning difficulties. Most of my subscores on the Wechsler were well above average, all two to three standard deviations above the norm. These subscores frame my gifts. On the Woodcock-Johnson, my broad reading score may have been 111 and at the 76th percentile, but my spelling and word attack were at the 37th percentile and my reading fluency and spelling of sounds were just over the 50th percentile. And this after 50 years of work trying to improve my reading performance. The only reason I was able to score at the 76th percentile in reading was my gifted passage comprehension at the

---

[2] Gifted Students With Learning Disabilities: Recommendations for Identification and Programming, M. Elizabeth Nielsen, *Exceptionality*, Jun 1, 2002, reprinted by permission of the publisher, Taylor & Francis Ltd, http://www.tandfonline.com

10 Definitions of Gifted, LD, and 2e

95th percentile. I would have scored much lower on the Figure 2.1 chart in reading if I did not have the high passage comprehension score.

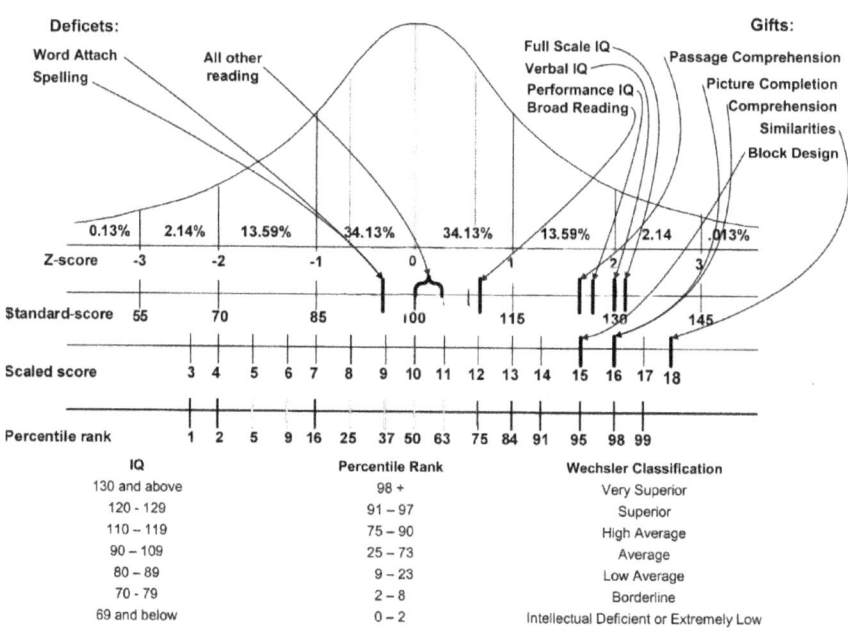

Figure 2.2 John Inman IQ chart with subdomains.

Learning deficits

Scholarly literature uses the terminology of learning disabilities, learning disorders, and learning deficits to describe learning deficits. As mentioned above, I have found learning deficits provides a more accurate description of my experience, but all three labels are used in the book. Researchers have not aligned behind one description, and if disability or disorder are used in common labels and literature, deficit reflects what I envision. A child with a specific learning deficit does not perform at the expected level in a specific academic domain for the age, ethnicity, culture, and so forth of the child. Specific learning disorders do not involve neurological or physical impairments. The American Psychological Association (APA) has refined its definition of specific learning disorders (disabilities) in the fifth edition of the Diagnostic and Statistical Manual of Mental Disorders (DSM-5) to reflect current thought on this field. Current language for specific learning disorders from the APA clarifies what specific learning disorders qualify and all those not qualifying (American Psychiatric Association, 2013):

> Characteristics of Specific Learning Disorder: Specific learning disorder is diagnosed through a clinical review of the individual's developmental, medical, educational, and family history, reports of test scores and teacher observations, and response to academic interventions. The diagnosis requires persistent difficulties in reading, writing, arithmetic, or mathematical reasoning skills during formal years of schooling. Symptoms may include inaccurate or slow and effortful reading, poor written expression that lacks clarity, difficulties remembering number facts, or inaccurate mathematical reasoning.
>
> Current academic skills must be well below the average range of scores in culturally and linguistically appropriate tests of reading, writing, or mathematics. The individual's difficulties must not be better explained by developmental, neurological, sensory (vision or hearing), or motor disorders and must significantly interfere with academic achievement, occupational performance, or activities of daily living:
>
> Because of the changes in DSM-5, clinicians will be able to make this diagnosis by identifying whether patients are unable to perform academically at a level appropriate to their intelligence and age. After a diagnosis, clinicians can provide greater detail into the type of deficit(s) that an individual has

through the designated specifiers. Just as in DSM-IV, dyslexia will be included in the descriptive text of specific learning disorder. The DSM-5 Neurodevelopmental Work Group concluded that the many definitions of dyslexia and dyscalculia meant those terms would not be useful as disorder names or in the diagnostic criteria. (p. 1)

Giftedness

"It is ironic that one of the most vexing questions in the field of gifted and talented education is how to define giftedness" (Subotnik, Olszewski-Kubilius, & Worrell, 2011, p. 7). Many perspectives represent the field and as the authors synthesized these perspectives into a working definition of giftedness, several themes emerged: (a) giftedness reflects the values of society; (b) actual outcomes in adulthood characterize giftedness; (c) define giftedness by domain as characteristics of giftedness do not necessarily manifest across all domains; (d) giftedness results from a combination of factors including biological, pedagogical, psychological, and psychosocial; and (e) the extraordinary relates to giftedness, not just the ordinary. For this book, I am using the following definition of *giftedness*. According to Subotnik, Olszewski-Kubilius, and Worrell:

> Giftedness is the manifestation of performance or production that is clearly at the upper end of the distribution in a talent domain even relative to that of other high-functioning individuals in that domain. Further, giftedness can be viewed as developmental, in that in the beginning stages, potential is the key variable; in later stages, achievement is the measure of giftedness; and in fully developed talents, eminence is the basis on which this label is granted. Psychosocial variables play an essential role in the manifestation of giftedness at every developmental

stage. Both cognitive and psychosocial variables are malleable and need to be deliberately cultivated. (p. 7)

Chapter 3
Indigenizing Mainstream Education

According to Four Arrows (2013), "Indigenizing mainstream education" refers to ways all teachers can learn to first question educational and cultural hegemony and then offer counterbalancing perspectives from the significantly different perspectives common to Indigenous approaches to teaching and learning. Doing this can lead to the proven results historically revealed in the abundant but too often oppressed literature revealing how the majority of Indigenous societies created healthy, happy, respectful, connected adults with the skills to survive and thrive and the dispositions for responsible, generous, and courageous action. Four Arrows aligns with current resilience theory and positive psychology. Brendtro and Larson (2004) state, "The goal is to support children as they develop courage to cope with the challenges and problems of life" (p. 194).

The work in this book does not attempt to speak for all Indigenous perspectives. In 2003 there were 562 recognized tribes in the United States (National Congress of American Indians, n.d.), 617 tribes/bands from 50 Nations in Canada (Aboriginal Affairs and Northern Development Canada, Government of Canada, n.d.) and close to 600 tribes in Mexico, Central, and South America (International Work Group for Indigenous Affairs, n.d.). Indigenous languages still spoken in the Americas exceed 1,000. As I continue to explore Indigenizing education, I do not assume I represent all these individual cultures. Common threads exist and I rely primarily upon the work of Four Arrows and Greg Cajete for identifying those that relate to my arguments.

Although I am not Indigenous nor an Indigenous scholar, this research conversation about drawing from Indigenous learning principles to help educate 2e children assists educators to move toward providing 2e children with an engaging and respectful educational experience. Four Arrows (2014) states, "My proposition that non-Indian teachers begin to Indigenize their courses by incorporating and comparing the two worldviews does not require expertise in Indigenous worldviews" (p. 43). Teaching Indigenous values and cultures, while important, does not give a non-Indigenous educator the appropriate tools to Indigenize a classroom. However, using Indigenous learning principles and historical accounts to provide contrasting views of history does enrich learning settings and improve the critical thinking and creativity of children. Indigenous educational principles, regardless of the tribal source embrace the differences each individual brings to the learning journey and provide consistently holistic and respectful learning environments (Cajete, 1994). This book defines the principles outlined in detail in Cajete, chapter 16, as they relate to my autoethnography. Thus, as I tell my story of how I dealt with dominant cultural perspectives, I *imagine* how different things might have been if the Indigenous perspectives on teaching and learning would have been prevailing.

In the Indigenous perspective, all of life on earth is a gift in all its variety. However, I did not experience growing up as gifted which is common for 2e children. I only discovered my gifts after I asked for an assessment before starting my doctoral program. My interest in helping other 2e children was born after I learned I had grown up as a 2e child. Interest in exploring educational strategies for both gifted and learning-disabled children continues to increase in the educational industry as well.

With the increased interest in 2e education, educators are looking for creative solutions to help 2e children and may be receptive to Indigenous learning principles to help 2e children learn. Researchers have found one of the roadblocks to innovation in the field to be a lack of conversation between educators of gifted and LD children. Those teaching LD children often do not talk to those who teach gifted children. The lack of conversation results in 2e children unrecognized as gifted ending up shuffled into remedial settings ignoring their gifts (Bracamonte, 2010; Brulles & Winebrenner, 2009; Winebrenner & Brulles, 2008; Yssel, Adams, Clarke, & Jones, 2014). According to Leggett, Shea, and Wilson (2010), "Although learning disabilities and giftedness both fall under the umbrella of special education services, these areas have a history of operating as distinct and separate entities, as demonstrated by separate professional organizations and journals" (p. 2).

Indigenizing curriculum requires changing the context of the educational culture to include rich and inclusive Indigenous principles and history rather than only a linear Western context based on one right way of being and knowing. Indigenizing curriculum does not mean doing away with current strategies to mitigate the impact of learning disabilities or reducing the need to add advanced work for gifted children nor does it propose using only in-classroom strategies or only specialized schools. An Indigenous framework embraces all ways of knowing and connectively binds all of existence together, embraces dialogue, and builds from the strengths and special gifts each child brings to the world.

Such a perspective is also lauded by progressive educators like John Dewey who believed in children constructing their knowledge from experience. "Dewey argued that all knowledge . . . is social knowledge, the product of an interplay of experience, testing and experiment, observation, reflection, and conversation, the fruit of a myriad of thinkers and doers" (Boyte, 2009, p. 12). According to this school of thought, the teacher provides the context to embrace multiple pathways in the classroom. One such model often used in education is Gardner's multiple intelligences. (Baum, Viens, & Slatin, 2005). Other approaches with broad-based acceptance include several factor theories of multiple pathways such as Spearman's 2-factor model. These factor models focus on a general intellectual ability and specific abilities or talents in children. Children may exhibit specific abilities in such things as math, languages, or art. There are not a set number of specific abilities as they are limited only by available valid assessments of specific abilities. These assessments have been developed to help educators determine where children excel and where they do not excel and can form the foundation for different educational pathways to help children develop their strengths and mitigate their weaknesses.

For this book, I refer to these different models as multiple pathways and assume educators will use the assessments and models they are most comfortable with. The important consideration is the understanding that multiple pathways are important because when using them, educators avoid classrooms where each child conforms to a predetermined right way of being, leaving children who see the world differently feeling broken and in need of fixing. As Palmer (1998) states, "The point is not to 'get fixed' but to gain deeper understanding of the paradox of gifts and limits, the paradox of our mixed selves" (p. 72).

Gifted children, whether twice-exceptional or not, can see the complexities of a connected world and embrace the ambiguity of multiple ways of knowing (Song & Porath, 2011). The cognitive dissonance caused by having to embrace ambiguous worldviews and ways of knowing provides an excellent framework for creativity and intellectual growth. An Indigenous framework introduces an alternative to Western perspectives and ways of knowing into the educational context alongside Western perspectives, which provides a rich and compelling framework for gifted children to explore solutions situated in the current global environment rather than a world envisioned only by Western thinking.

I explore an Indigenous framework in this book hoping to create educational settings where 2e children can unleash their power and creativity: "if educators fulfill this obligation, they will unlock and unleash the great power within these students – and that will benefit them, their families, society, and the world in ways that cannot even be imagined" (Leggett, Shea, & Wilson, 2010, p. 8). Mark Sorensen, the headmaster of the STAR Navajo School, a school that draws from Indigenous learning foundations, provides an example of possible achievements that come from Indigenizing a school (Sorensen, 2013). Mr. Sorensen outlines the values of the STAR school and the successes realized for Navajo students. The values are (a) Service To All Relations which provides the foundation for the STAR name; (b) 4 R's which include Respect, Relationship, Responsibility, and Reasoning; (c) expecting excellence in the preparation of our students for life; (d) honoring our place and place-based education; and (e) to be in harmony with our environment. The STAR school provides a glimpse into a possible model for what an educational program for 2e children might look like if based on Indigenous learning foundations.

Chapter 4
Why This Research and a Plea for Change

I have explored my lived experience of being 2e juxtaposed with what my experience might have been within the context of Indigenous learning foundations. I largely glean from the works of Cajete (1994, 2005) and Four Arrows (2013). As a 2e learner, I experienced the impact of a linear Western worldview on someone not fitting the Western view of a normal child; that is a child who held the same worldview and way of knowing supported by mainstream education curriculum and school practices. I envision many if not most 2e and alternative learning children grow up with similar experiences to my less than positive experience growing up 2e. Based on my experience as a 2e learner and my research and recommended application of Indigenous learning foundations, I propose a dialogic and respectful approach to learning for 2e and alternative learning children. I use my story as a catalyst for improving the educational experience of 2e children. Although I specifically lived a 2e experience, the ideas proposed may have the same positive effect on other alternative learning children. We should expect more than contributions to the community from these children; they have the potential for creative leadership helping the world through future difficult transitions.

Who Are These Children?

According to the U.S. Department of Education (April 2013), 4.7% of children in the US receive services for specific learning disabilities with 5.9% of that population considered gifted (U.S. Department of Education, May 2008). However, a longitudinal study by Lovett and

Sparks (2011) of 48 2e researchers found variability in defining gifted. On average, the researchers considered about 10% of children gifted with a total IQ of 120 or above. Researchers estimate 2e children comprise about 2-5% of gifted children based on impartial data (Bracamonte, 2010), a number many believe underestimates the population of 2e children (Bracamonte; Nielsen, 2002, p. 94). According to the U.S. Department of Education (January 2013), 55,091,000 children attended public and private schools in the United States in 2012. Given this population, about 5 million gifted children attended school in 2012. A quick calculation would indicate more than 250,000 children fall at the intersection of these two populations, the 2e children. Assouline, Foley Nicpon, and Huber (2006) estimate this number to be closer to 360,000.

Mainstream Western educational classrooms often overlook the gifts of 2e children. Examples of gifts include creative thinking, unusual imagination, understanding of complex relations and systems, good problem-solving, penetrating insights, and highly developed intuition (Song & Porath, 2011). As a result of being overlooked, 2e children often land in remedial learning programs along with other alternative learning children (Baum, 2004; Baum & Owen, 2004; Lovecky, 2004; Webb et al., 2005; Winebrenner, 2003). These 2e children do not have an opportunity to realize their potential when educators focus on remedial solutions designed to fix them. Educators should instead focus on developing the gifts of 2e children. Alternative learning children simply do not learn the way Western education wants them to learn as twice-exceptional children do not fit well into a Western learning framework.

Educators need to experience a mindset shift to move from a Western worldview perspective to a Western and Indigenous worldview perspective. Where Indigenous values include a focus on being, community relationships, living in the present, and harmony with the world, Western values include a focus on doing, individuality, a future time frame, and mastery over nature (Garrett, 1999). Bringing educators into a conversation to explore how to co-create a new path forward based on both worldviews must be the focus of conversations focused on 2e educational reform. The foundation of this conversation includes the belief that every child brings gifts to be developed. An Indigenous foundation first and foremost provides a context for the healing belief that every unique and special child requires no fixing (Cajete, 1994). The expected norm in Western education frames interventions without a foundation such as described above. Often Western educators mold those children who do not meet the norm to fit the Western context. One root of this practice comes from the definition of normal derived from the *Diagnostic and Statistical Manual* (DSM) used by psychologists to determine if someone is abnormal. The DSM "uses statistical standards of normal to label those deemed abnormal" (Brendtro & Larson, 2004, p. 199). In other words, if a child does not fit the definition of normal, the child becomes abnormal and needs fixing.

I explore an educational paradigm focusing on developing healthy, creative, and intelligent alternative learning children who have the potential of making a substantial contribution to the world. Given the challenges faced in k-12 education, I propose a conversation about transforming current educational approaches from a dualistic Western-only worldview to a holistic worldview introducing Indigenous learning foundations, which embrace complexity to define the world in which we now live. Hassan (2014) states the opportunity:

> In the past, everything was less connected. Today, interconnectivity is rapidly increasing, creating an age defined by its complexity. This connectivity has many dividends, but it also means that our landscape of challenges has changed dramatically in the last few decades. In the past, problems could be dealt with in isolation, while today, most of our most intractable social challenges are deeply interconnected. They don't respect man-made boundaries, such as national borders.

The nature of interconnectivity means that we are seeing challenges that are entirely new *and* fast changing. (p. 20)

Creating a Sense of Urgency to Address This Gap

I hope my lived experience juxtaposed with how this experience might have played out in an Indigenous setting sparks a conversation on how to approach teaching children differently: not only 2e children, but all alternative learning children, and if possible all children. We can expect children to continue to grow up in complexity and a challenging world. Twice-exceptional children possessing alternative ways of knowing, learning, and seeing the world feel at home in the world of complexity (Bracamonte, 2010). The Western mindset demanding "one size fits all" does not fully prepare students to address complexity, uncertainty, and ambiguity, the norm in the emerging world. The mechanistic and dualistic Western approach to the world lacks the mental models necessary to thrive in the current environment of complexity. "Conventional top-down teaching does not prepare students well for the realities of that world" (Palmer, 1998, p. 179). By supplementing an educational setting based on the dualistic mindset with Indigenous models, a learning environment emerges embracing different ways of knowing and providing multiple learning pathways.

I consider the conversations taking place at the intersection between Western alternative learning programs and Indigenous learning foundations borderland conversations. The borderlands (Kincheloe & Steinberg, 2008) between these worldviews provide the fertile ground for rich and engaging conversations to emerge. Applying borderlands epistemology to alternative learner program development as an innovation provides a deeper understanding of what happens when competing worldviews come together. Just as cultures collide at their borders, so do worldviews. New cultures and non-envisioned possibilities emerge at these borderlands.

Comparison of Two Types of Living

	Small-band gatherer-hunters	United States Today
Social embeddedness	High	Low
Social support	High	Low
Socially purposeful living	Normative	Non-normative
Community social enjoyment	Every day	Rare (spectator sports, religious services)
Boundaries	Fluid, companionship/kinship culture	Rigid kinship culture, social classes
Physical contact with others	Considerable (sleep, rest, dance, song)	Minimal
Relations with other groups	Cooperative	Competitive attitude, cooperative action
Individual freedom	Extensive, no coercion	Free to make consumption choices if adult, coercion
Relationships	Egalitarian (no one bosses anyone)	Hierarchical
Contact with other ages	Multi-age group living day and night	Rare outside of family home
Role models	Virtuous Frequently	Vicious within popular media
Cultural mores	Generosity and cooperation are fostered & expected	Selfishness and stubbornness fostered and expected
Immorality	Cheating, abuse, aggression not tolerated	Cheating, abuse, aggression expected
Natural world	Embeddedness/ in partnership with Nature	Detachment from, control and fear of Nature

Figure 4.1 Comparison of Indigenous vs. Western living. Four Arrows & Narvaez, 2014

Borderland conversations between worldviews found within alternative learner program development and Indigenous learning create a mixing or cross-pollination process or a creolization process (Cohen & Toninato, 2010; Pieterse, 2009). The Indigenous model sees complementarity as a main defining quality of all nature. On the contrary, competition and hierarchy are more common in the dominant worldview-based cultures. Using creolization to explain interactions at the borderlands helps overcome the dualistic outcome of a right or wrong perspective. Participants with different worldviews in conversations can co-create something altogether new at the borderland, something drawing from the strengths of both Western and Indigenous worldviews. To do this requires a shift from the dualistic right or wrong mindset to an altered consciousness where we can begin to see new possibilities not fitting within the old worldviews. This altered consciousness with a feeling of interconnectedness to other states known as the liminal (Campbell, 1972) develops when the participants hold mindsets at the boundary and at the same time embrace both sides of the boundary. The liminal emerges in the state between the starting mindsets and the ending mindset and provides the temporary state where participants in the conversation have suspended solidified worldviews and willingly work together to co-create a new worldview: In this case, a worldview creating a better learning environment for 2e children.

The liminal closely associates with borderlands epistemology. For a new worldview to emerge from differing worldviews colliding at the borderland, a liminal state must exist. When we structure conversations at the borderland correctly, the liminal can emerge, mindsets can shift, and we can alter our course forward to honor multiple perspectives. The sooner we create borderland conversations to co-create a new way forward for 2e education, the sooner we can reduce or eliminate the damage being done to 2e children.

As we cannot go back in history and waiting allows the damage done by existing paradigms to continue, educators must act now to explore a new approach founded on developing capabilities through the addition of Indigenous models to teaching both 2e children and other children who have alternative learning needs or ways of knowing. We need a community to come together in conversation to plan, to solve problems, to chart a course forward in complex environments, and to deal with conflict provides a foundation for Indigenous learning to enter the conversation. The Universal Design for Learning (UDL) movement has provided a model of how these conversations can be initiated with the support of the community, teachers, parents, and school administration.

Human ability to effectively address increasing challenges has not kept pace with the rate of change in the world. To understand complexity, people of all ages and backgrounds must engage in conversations about questions critical to the health and well-being of not only the individuals in the community but the community as a whole. In Indigenous frameworks, spirit provides the center of concentric rings radiating out first through individuals, then to families, then to communities, and finally out to the world. Conversations start in spirit and always look out to the world. Indigenous models support this dialogic framework (Cajete, 1994; Four Arrows, 2013) as does the prominent 2e researcher Diane Montgomery (2003) addressing the necessity of adding talking techniques into curricula for 2e children. The practice of dialogue illustrates one of the primary differences in Western and Indigenous perspectives.

The infusion of dialogue into 2e education provides a critical step in creating talking strategies. Conversations between people certainly highlight an aspect of dialogue and an important one. However, dialogue between people and their world provides an expanded foundation for an Indigenous worldview. Figure 4.1 (Four Arrows & Narvaez, 2015) provides an example of how Western and Indigenous worldviews differ and, the co-creation of the world through dialogue with the world around the community. These comparisons are idealized and attempt to explain basic worldviews. They are not intended to suggest all Indigenous social constructs are positive and all Western social constructs are negative. Virtue and evil are found in the actual manifestation of both worldviews. Articulation of each can provide the foundation of a conversation at the borderlands where the two collide. Articulating the basic assumptions underlying the two worldviews will help frame inquiry at the borderlands to better understand how each impact learning for 2e children. Co-creation of a new reality based on this conversation provides the power for real change to emerge. One of the evils demonstrated by those individuals embedded in either worldview comes from the tendency to demonize the other's views. Only through dialogue at the borderlands where these worldviews collide will this dysfunction be replaced with a new path forward. While theorists and practitioners wait for solutions to ongoing challenges to materialize, pressing global issues persist or even accelerate. Solutions emerge out of conversation, not a simple transmission of existing knowledge. Communication emerges through co-creating a better world with those around us, not through transferring pre-existing information to others (Pearce, 2007; Pearce, 2009b).

We need to explore alternative ways of teaching 2e children based on Indigenous dialogic foundations to develop healthy and whole people who can help heal the world. Taylor and Van Every (2008) make this point when they say, "through conversation, collectively interacting individuals produce an emergent knowledge, which is not merely the sum of their joint contributions but arises out of the dynamics of interconnection" (p. 241).

Hope for the Future

As this book does not intend to provide proof for a theory of education, learning will emerge based on the meaning the reader constructs during the process of exploring my lived experience and my considerations of how Indigenous learning foundations might have made a difference. Thus, this book explores my story and my insights as to how I would have learned if I had been exposed to an Indigenous learning framework. My story depends on what I might have learned and the context of my learning. The multiple histories and experiences of people and the world would have been engaging additions to my education, and a context embracing multiple ways of knowing would have created a learning environment where I might have felt accepted and special. Having conversations about the material and concepts in my courses rather than having data presented in a lecture would have transformed my learning.

My experience growing up and living as a 2e learner has been challenging, and I have often wished I could have experienced education differently. This book provides me with the opportunity to explore alternative learning settings where Indigenous learning principles enrich the curriculum. I hope an opportunity for a new approach to educating 2e and alternative learning children becomes apparent as readers of this story join me on the journey to develop whole human beings where despair, disillusionment, and doubt now frame the experience of so many children.

Part Two
My Journey
An Autoethnography

*"Everyone has to find the right path.
You can't see it so it's hard
to find. No one can show you. Each
person has to find the path
by himself."*
-- -- Charlie Knight, UTE

Chapter 5
A Brief Autobiographical Sketch

In Indigenous traditions, it is common to introduce yourself by identifying your place in the world through an explanation of who your family is. I will follow that tradition. I trace my Inman family to the 1400s in Chester, England. In researching my wife's and my family genealogy, I have identified over 10,000 individuals in our combined family tree. My genetic family consists wholly of White European ancestry; specifically, all come from the British Isles. Although my mother's mother believed she had a Cherokee great-grandmother, my research currently does not confirm this. I found one possible link, Captain John Martindale, a cavalry unit of one for the Confederate Army during the Civil War. He married and lived in Cherokee territory, but I have no record of his wife's lineage. John Martindale would be my grandfather several times removed. My research confirms my family as English, Irish, Welsh, and Scottish. Most immediately I have Joyce (Irish) heritage from my mother and Inman (English) heritage from my father.

With all of this said, I do not believe bloodline makes a family. Indigenous populations have a long history of adopting people of all backgrounds into the tribe. My sister's children came to the family through adoption and my wife's siblings came to her family through adoption. They belong in the family every bit as much as anyone else. In my immediate family, my daughter, an unmistakable Inman, comes from a proud and ancient Telugu heritage from south India. In doing genealogical research, children and wives commonly join families through adoption when unexpected death or adversity strikes a family. I have found this often in my family research.

I was the third child born to Geraldine Louise Joyce and Louis Howard Inman. I was a surprise to older parents, my brother being 19 years older and my sister 14 years older. All are now passed. As my siblings were older, I grew up as an only child as Jerry and Joyce were young adults living away from home before I started school.

Growing up in the shadow of an older brother who was a diplomat, fluent in Spanish and Japanese, and successful throughout his career, challenged me as a 2e child. Learning came easy to Jerry, and my trials and tribulations were probably odd to him. I always felt Jerry did not understand my challenges. We never had a lot of time together and I struggled to gain a sense of efficacy in his shadow. Each struggle experienced was met with questions about my decisions. How I longed for a sympathetic ear and an accepting response from a big brother who was old enough to be my father. I understand his generation, the traditional generation, which was born before 1945. They had a different cultural outlook and experience than boomers like me. This may account for his mindset. I learned to let my feelings of inadequacy in the shadow of my brother go over the years. Many of these struggles were directly related to growing up 2e and some to having a brother 19 years older who grew up in a world I did not recognize.

My parents provided a stable family. They were kind, loving, and married 60 years before my father passed at age 84. My mother passed in 2012 at age 100. Both of my parents were loved by members of their community. They lived during a time of lifelong employment and stable social structures. I have not experienced this level of stability, which accounts for much of my disconnection over the years.

I cannot blame my struggles and decisions on upbringing or socioeconomics. My twice-exceptionality was given to me by the Creator, a gift I have had to learn how to use. It has taken me 67 years to figure this gift out. I was blessed with my wife, Hazel, who stuck with me through so much over our 35 years of marriage. She provided my strongest support when the world seems to be crumbling around me. We have two children. I find it interesting both our children and my wife are strong in language arts, and my second exceptionality is dyslexia. I am the slowest reader in the family, my writing the worst, and my ability to learn language the poorest. In an oral tradition, these challenges would have disappeared. I suspect I am strongest, however, in my ability to synthesize disparate inputs into creative solutions or persist in the face of adversity. My gift of twice-exceptionality gives me these talents.

In no way do I equate my experience with minority experiences or experiences of those who have physical or mental impairments, yet I do have deep empathy for those who do not fit into the norm in our culture. My empathy for the experiences of others also comes from my gift of twice-exceptionality. My empathy for those who see and approach the world differently drew me to the study of Indigenous learning cultures where the dualistic right/wrong paradigm found in Western cultures fades.

As I reflect on the family I have been blessed with and my experience growing up 2e, I can only wonder about how others who have never experienced 2e see me and others like me. Western culture does not readily accept those not fitting neatly into the expectations of society. I feel as though I am viewed with suspicion if I attempt to address or explain my twice-exceptionality. Invariably when I attempt to explain my experience, the response is something like, "I switch letters and words sometimes too." I have found no way to describe my 2e journey to someone who has not lived the experience of growing up as a 2e person. The experience of feeling I do not fit in would have been eliminated had I experienced the acceptance inherent in a place-based culture, particularly since I have moved around in location and profession so much. Those years of effort would have been far better invested in developing my strengths rather than trying to conform to Western norms. Growing up with an Indigenous learning foundation would have been life-changing if for no other reason than creating a strong sense of efficacy and self-esteem. Each 2e child growing up in a system where they are viewed as broken and in need of fixing will experience a similar result of having their gifts ignored and years of effort focused instead on overcoming their weaknesses.

Chapter 6
Early Reading Problems

Early reading issues are one of the most common learning challenges twice-exceptional children like me face. The language educator's use about developmental difficulties in spelling and reading contributes to the learning environment 2e children experience. Although educators often treat dyslexia as a medical condition, this misclassification creates challenges for 2e children. My research has helped me to understand I do not have a medical condition. Twice-exceptional children's brains process differently; they do not have a disease or medical deformity. Learning strategies then are critical to the development of 2e children, not medically inspired interventions. Embracing non-dualistic approaches such as Indigenizing the classroom and adding strategies from Indigenous learning foundations offer important changes to classrooms to help 2e children like me learn.

My K-5 Experience

I grew up with reading difficulties in a learning system founded on reading rather than oral traditions. There was no flexibility to provide me with different learning pathways as would have been the case in an Indigenous learning environment. I would have thrived in such a dialogic environment based on learning through experience, collaboration, stories, and complex, real-life scenarios. My sense of efficacy and my self-esteem would not have been so damaged in the process. I certainly would not have ended up graduating from fifth-grade unable to read first-grade material and thinking I was stupid. I would have been on my way to becoming a whole and healthy human being. Instead at the end of fifth-grade, I simply could not read well. My school experience was like the experience 2e children often face now, 55 years later. Unfortunately, in many settings, things have not changed much. I think the complexity and demands of overstretched school systems have been a roadblock to the transformation of how we teach 2e children. As well, isolated solutions implemented without an understanding of the whole system invariably fail and expert-based solutions created without a deep conversation between all involved including the children often lead to uninspired and inadequate solutions. Rather than trying to tackle the whole system, a more targeted approach using cluster-grouped classrooms (see chapter 14 for a closer look at cluster grouping) combined with Indigenous principles may help

Figure 6.1 Lytton School in Palo Alto, CA where John Inman experienced his first six years of school.

with the transition. The structural social injustice will not change without altering how educators look at 2e learning which will help remove the roadblocks in the current culture.

I have scant memories of my early school experience. I remember the old multistory wooden Lytton Schoolhouse in Palo Alto, CA where I experienced my first 6 years of school. I remember nap time in kindergarten on my little blanket in the basement and running up and down the wooden stairs. I remember kickball and dodgeball in the playground, my friends, and bullies. I also remember always sitting at the back of the room hoping and praying the teacher would not notice me or call on me. But I remember little else about the educational experience, with two exceptions. I was so traumatized by the introduction of School Mathematics Study Group (SMSG), new math, I still can tell you exactly what the books looked and felt like. They were paperback yellow books with a rough texture. I remember with terror the confusion and bewilderment I felt trying to understand what to me was a foreign language. My father, a scientist, mathematician, and electrical engineer could not even help me understand it. This math experiment in California school systems lived only a short while. Unfortunately, I was in the middle of the experiment.

After my encounter with SMSG, not only could I not read, I could not understand math, and my fear of math followed me into adulthood. Ironically, I am quite good at math; I just never learned I was good at math as I was so intimidated by it. I have no problem with math when teachers teach math situated in nature, in current experiences, or explored through arts. Genetics in college was easy for me as was statistical process control when I was a quality consultant. I see patterns and enjoy solving problems. Had an Indigenous learning framework been in place during my first 6 years of school, math would have been learned through real-life application and integration with the natural world rather than trying to memorize and learn formulas and concepts with little connection to my reality as a child.

I also remember band where I tried to learn the clarinet, certainly a better experience than math. I loved both the clarinet and singing. It was difficult for me to remember the music and read the musical scores for the clarinet, but I had fun trying. The one educational experience I remember from grade school is music, a subject included in one of the seven Indigenous learning foundations. I can even remember the look and feel of the clarinet I used. I was so proud to bring the instrument home and practice. Unfortunately,

40 Early Reading Problems

music also becomes one of the first subjects to be cut by school districts during a budget crisis.

During these formative years, I found myself in a learning environment ignoring my inability to read and crippling my ability

Figure 6.2 Second-grade class at Lytton School, Palo Alto, CA.

to learn math. When I should have been developing a love of learning and developing my gifts, I learned instead to fear school and dread the experience of feeling stupid. Had an Indigenous framework been in place, I would have felt part of a learning community, encouraged to dream and connect with the learning, my gifts would have been embraced, and I would have felt nurtured and accepted. My creative brain would have thrived on creating stories, learning from myths, and experiencing math through art and a connection with the world around me, all Indigenous approaches to learning. Educators create a profound impact not only on 2e children but on our culture and world. When children experience what I experienced growing up as 2e, the power teachers have to create a better world is diminished. When I could have been accelerating and living into my potential, instead I struggled with fears, uncertainties, and doubts about who I was and what I could contribute. When I look back on friends who went through the same school system, they seem to have thrived and gained mastery of their work and fields of practice. To this day I find it difficult to understand how it can be so easy for others when I struggle. I have as hard a time empathizing with the learning experience of others as they do with me. Outside of school, I was always on an equal or advanced level with my friends. Like many 2e children, I thrived outside of the classroom, not in the classroom.

During the summer after second grade, I had the opportunity to have an extraordinary experience outside of the classroom. My parents arranged a trip for me to spend a summer on my

Figure 6.3 Grandparents' farm in Mansfield, AR.

grandparents' farm in Mansfield, Arkansas, my mother's childhood home, an experience having a profound impact on me as I grew up. It was the summer before my eighth birthday and my third-grade year. Looking back on this experience, I suspect I was a bit young for such an excursion from Palo Alto to Mansfield by myself. I did not know my grandparents; I think I had met them once or twice. My parents put me on a plane to Arkansas with a friend of theirs, and off I went. The farm was a 400-acre working farm in the Ozarks my grandfather and his four sons cleared by hand. The house had been built before the Civil War and was held together by square nails. I was fascinated by the house, the farm, the yard, the crops; in fact, I was fascinated by everything there. I welcomed the

Figure 6.4 John Inman on the farm in Mansfield, AR.

opportunity of getting away from the discouragement of school and onto the farm. I loved animals and being outdoors on the farm provided me with a learning framework that might have come right out of an Indigenous learning platform. I was outdoors every day. I learned about the animals, collected eggs from the chickens, milked the cows, and helped in the large garden my grandmother harvested from for canning. Many 2e children like me thrive outside of the classroom in experiential activities building on their strengths. My feet toughened up so I could go barefoot most of the time. I felt like I was learning to be part of the earth, plants, and animals. The dogs were my best friends, and my grandmother protected me from my grandfather's violent outbursts just as she did with my mother. I watched my grandparents and learned farming from them. I learned the names of the insects; the cicadas were my favorite. I had numerous close calls with scorpions and a run-in with a copperhead snake in the cornfield. My grandmother came out and killed it with

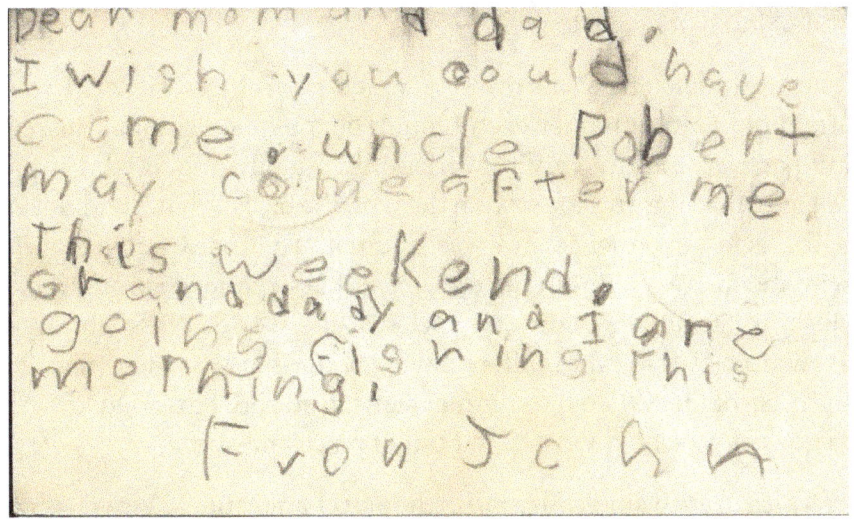

Figure 6.5 John Inman note home 8/20/1960.

a hoe. I still remember the dirt between my toes; it was hot and just like powder. We ate fresh vegetables every day and I got to dig up peanuts and roast them. This was a learning environment I thrived in. It was experiential, something my grade school did not provide. This learning environment harkened back to my forefathers and Indigenous peoples and how they lived for thousands of years. The one difference, for the Indigenous peoples, there was a spiritual connection to the land, the plants, the animals, and the community. Most Westerners probably did not bring this reverence with them. My experience created a spiritual connection with the world around me which has stayed with me my whole life.

In Figure 6.5, I show a note home to my parents demonstrating my dysgraphia. Dysgraphia commonly accompanies dyslexia and is not a result of not trying to write. I was taught to write cursive and spent countless hours trying to write well. To this day, writing is difficult for me and I print in all caps when I write and do not attempt to write cursive. I simply cannot translate what is in my head to my hand unless it is gross motor skills, with which I am accomplished. I am always amazed at those who can draw, write, and paint. It is magic to me.

Unfortunately, not all my stay was a perfect experience. I was afraid of my grandfather even though he took me fishing. I missed my parents, and my very best friend, the family dog, died. I went out one morning and found him dead on the back porch. I had never had a death experience and was traumatized. That trauma stayed with me for years. But in the end, even that experience brought me closer to an understanding of cycles of the world. When children grow up closer to nature, they have a better sense of their place in the cycle of life. When the summer came to an end, I dreaded having to go back to school where I felt out of place and stupid.

Third, fourth, and fifth grades did not change much. I was falling further and further behind, with little hope in sight. The wasted potential, the wasted learning, the wasted self-esteem—I am amazed I made it out of these early years at all. I also imagine how I might have avoided the demoralization completely had I been in an Indigenous learning environment. The environment would have been far more experiential; I would have learned orally and found my place in the world. I never would have felt broken. Even now at 67, I have a hard time imagining what it would feel like not to be broken. This has been a pervasive part of my life. No child should have to go through this type of experience. Each child has the right to be nurtured and guided to realize their potential. The cultural cost must be extraordinary. Having managed and developed hundreds of employees in my career, many struggling with many of the same issues I struggle with, I can see the staggering cost to organizations and society. This cost will not be addressed using dualistic approaches to problem-solving. The expert model falls short in addressing the complexities of education for 2e children. I suspect we will see progress with a systems view of everything going on and a dialogic approach to help those with different worldviews come together to co-create solutions making a difference in children's lives. Only by working together and breaking down barriers will transformation emerge.

As I look at my k-5 story, I find it interesting I remember so few details of my school experience. Yet outside of school, I remember so much. During this time, when children are taught to learn and love to learn, I became fearful of school and blocked out most of the experience. What I have written reflects those pieces of my learning life most striking to me. In talking with others, it amazes me how they remember their teachers and especially those teachers having a positive impact on their lives. I simply have no such memories. I do not remember classroom experiences or teachers through my college experience. I have no good or bad memories; I simply remember feeling unsuccessful in school. I also find my recollection of learning away from school interesting. I never would have realized how much I learned away from the classroom had I not experienced research into my 2e learning. The act of writing this story has helped me understand my k-5 experience as a child.

The culture I grew up in was so different than the one I now experience. Those were the boom years; prosperity was accelerating, and it might have been considered an idyllic time. I was a happy and active child when out of school. The world was stable outside of the constant threat of a nuclear attack or an earthquake. Yes, I do remember the drills. Change was slow and manageable. Children who could not thrive in school could make a good living in a trade and still enjoy the American dream of owning a house and retiring. Having my gifts ignored created discouragement but would not have blocked me from excelling in a profession where academics were unnecessary. However, with the current culture, the story does not play out well for 2e children. The rapid rate of knowledge and technology expansion boggles the mind. Real income levels for non-knowledge workers are declining. Escalation of prices for everything has outstripped wages. Depressing a child's potential in the current culture has a completely different outcome than it did 55 years ago. When schools now ignore the gifts of children, when they block the potential of children, they are crippling the ability of these children to fully participate in the world.

Schools operating as factories trying to turn out children who all have similar learning paths harken back to an approach born in a world that no longer exists. In the current culture of volatility, uncertainty, complexity, and ambiguity, children must believe in their ability to be a positive force in the world and be developed to do so, or they will be unequipped to participate fully in the emerging world. The social injustice of wealth disparity will only increase if we do not address transforming the learning experiences of 2e and other alternative learning children. Solutions born out of closed conversations between a few experts will most likely fall short in eliminating social injustice. The problems cannot be addressed by those who are integral to the problem and believe they can stand back and objectively see solutions. The lack of an integrated solution can only be solved through deep dialogue at the borderlands with those with differing worldviews.

Through my research into my experience as a 2e person, I have developed an appreciation for others who are either 2e or have alternative learning pathways. I often explore in conversation what others have experienced or in the case of children, what their experiences are currently. This connection with others has helped me feel a connection lacking over the years. Others who have had similar experiences understand my journey. I do not have to justify or explain my experience to other alternative learning individuals; they just get it. This connection with other 2e and alternative learning individuals has been one of the most rewarding parts of my learning journey. The experience of connection cannot be created by outside experts, it can only be socially constructed through conversation with others who have had similar experiences to mine.

Chapter 7
Middle School Years: Another 5th Grade and Private School

I was 11 years old in 1963 when I graduated fifth-grade from Lytton community school, just a block from my home. All my childhood friends I grew up with were there; it was my life. When I completed fifth-grade, I was tested for reading, and they found I could barely read first-grade material. One of the teachers must have been astute enough to flag this out for my parents. I suspect it was my fifth-grade English teacher. I had memorized lessons and had other children help me get through school. The teachers let me pass through. My feeling of being stupid got worse and worse as I grew older. Why could everyone else get all the lessons but not me? Teachers treated me as though I was lazy and not bright. I was a nice kid, did not create trouble, and they liked me, so I was somewhat out of mind. I suspect they knew there was something wrong, but they did not have time or skills to deal with it.

I was like many 2e children; I did not perform so poorly to be put in remedial programs but performed just well enough to meet the minimum grade standards. I used my gifts to compensate for my deficits. When 2e children are ready for sixth grade where the schoolwork becomes more complex and they can no longer compensate for deficits (not a conscious effort) by using their gifts, they begin to fail. So Lytton School just let things go until my parents were alerted to the prognosis, I could not read and would fail going forward. I was put through batteries of tests, EEG tests, intelligence tests, and saw a series of psychologists. I felt like a lab rat. What was wrong with me? The professionals all said I was smart but just did not apply myself. I was broken and needed fixing and the public schools were in no position to help, particularly mine. I was blessed that my parents were ready and committed to helping me.

I am indebted to my parents. My father was a scientist who never made a lot of money and my mother was a homemaker. I grew up loved in a stable family and had no excuse for my lack of ability to read. No one had a label for me, I just could not read. Dyslexia was not a term commonly in use at the time. My parents did not accuse me of being lazy as my teachers had; they simply believed in me and started a quest to find a place where I could learn to learn and read. We decided to enroll me at Ford Country Day School (FCDS) in Los Altos Hills, CA in the spring of 1963, and the most important reason for this was Brent Warner. Brent Warner was the owner and the youngest headmaster of a private school in the nation. He was

Figure 7.1 Ford Country Day School, Los Altos Hills, CA.

convinced his staff would turn my learning experience around. He agreed to allow my mother to drive children to school to help pay for my tuition as my parents could not afford what was being charged.

As I look back on my experience preceding Ford Country Day School, I cannot say I did not learn, and I cannot say life lessons have not served me. I felt I had to work harder to overcome obstacles than most around me and my inherent perseverance helped me make it through the first 6 years of school at Lytton, lessons that have benefited me my whole life. Had Indigenous learning principles been in place, I would have been putting my perseverance to work to help me realize my potential rather than survive in a world that seemed to be orchestrated against my way of being.

Brent asked my parents to hold me back and start fifth-grade again. Then he and his staff started me on a lifelong journey of a passion for learning. I never felt I could learn before the four years at FCDS. The work at FCDS was grueling for me. I was determined to learn how to learn and my teachers were always patient with me. Everyone around me seemed smart. As I observed them, lessons and schoolwork seemed easy for them. I felt humbled to be able to be in a school with such smart kids. I worked hard and slowly I began to learn to read and to learn. I felt like I was on a little protected island in the world. The staff did not call me stupid or lazy. I made friends. I felt accepted. It still brings tears to my eyes as I remember this experience. It was one of the only times in my life I have truly felt at home when away from my family.

My memories, unlike those for k-5, are rich and compelling from my 5-8 experience at FCDS. What was it about my experience helping me to learn? My teachers were unschooled in Indigenous learning nor were they schooled in cluster grouping education. This was a private school with teachers selected by Brent Warner specifically for their ability to transform learning for children. As this was one of the target schools in the San Francisco Bay Area for wealthy families to send their children, the standards of teaching were higher than my public grade school and probably higher than the most public grade schools. Otherwise, Brent would not have been able to attract families and their children to the school.

I have often wondered what my teachers did differently at FCDS. I do not remember the details. Why were they successful in transforming my life when my teachers at Lytton could not? It was not only the class size as in some of my Lytton pictures, we also had small classes. I think it may have been that the FCDS teachers self-selected out of the public schools because they too did not fit the norm. They did things differently, they thought differently, and they wanted to be in an environment allowing them to innovate. I will never know exactly what was different, but it was different. It seems to me parents are looking for alternatives to public schools more interested in test scores than in learning. The culture in the United States contributes to the problem. Public schools must balance keeping the voting public happy through a focus on testing and at the same time keep a focus on learning for the children. These do not have to be mutually exclusive; however, private schools seem to have far more flexibility in focusing on learning than public schools do. In private schools, parents vote with their pocketbooks. If the school does not create high levels of learning, the parents take their children to another school. Unfortunately, most public-school children and families do not have the resources to make this move, nor are there available schools. The transformation of education for 2e children therefore must happen in public schools and not be relegated to special schools where 99% of children are excluded. Social injustice will not be eliminated until this change happens.

I remember this about my teachers and experiences at FCDS. Some of the foundational principles of learning from Indigenous learning platforms were probably integral to Brent's philosophy and the teachers he selected. Teachers treated each of us as if we had gifts. We received special attention matched to our learning needs. We were encouraged, expected, and guided to perform. We had a rich assortment of activities including art, sports, choir, theater, and language arts. We had beautiful grounds and a natural setting to experience. Granted the disciplines were unintegrated, but they were a valuable and integral part of our learning. The class size was

Figure 7.2 Eighth-grade graduating class at FCDS (John Inman upper left).

small, and teachers took a real interest in our success. All these principles would also be synonymous with an Indigenous learning environment. The difference would be we can add these same strategies into a public-school setting and provide these opportunities outside of a high-priced private school if we integrate Indigenous strategies into cluster-grouped classrooms. I would not have needed a private school setting to learn to read and learn if these strategies had been integral to Lytton School.

I probably would not have had continuing education in my future without my FCDS experience. I can only imagine the pain and fright other children feel without parents who are willing or able to sacrifice so much as my parents did to help me. I have talked with many parents who were trying to do the right thing for their 2e children but were faced with school systems lacking the will or capacity to help their children. In every case, these families knew their children had gifts and the school systems did not acknowledge 2e as an explanation. Only after our conversation does the light bulb go on for these parents and they finally understand the challenges their children face. The schools are failing these families and children. My heart breaks to see this pattern continuing 55 years after my experience growing up 2e.

I do not know the statistics, but I imagine few children are given the chance my parents gave me. The question I ask is, what do we need to be doing differently to ensure every 2e child can learn in a healthy and supportive learning environment? The addition of Indigenous learning principles might help educators develop a mindset where teachers do not allow 2e children to languish. Then policy, processes, and programs will follow but only through dialogue and embracing different perspectives. Had educators used this strategy with me through the years, I would have felt like I too had gifts. If teachers had connected me to the world, nurtured my ability to engage in conversation with others, helped me to dream and to take ownership for my power to make positive changes in the world, my life would have been transformed. Teachers can provide these gifts to 2e children, transforming their lives, and creating change agents going forth to provide creative solutions to reverse the challenges humanity has created.

Parent and educator circumstances contribute to the social injustice created in school systems. A lack of time and resources available to parents in the current culture creates a challenge. My father, although only earning a low salary, was able to create a future for his family. My mother did not work outside of the home and took care of the family. When my father was my age, he was retired. He also had a pension. Most families in the United States currently have two parents working to make ends meet and have less time or disposable income to invest in alternative education for their children. Single-family households are on the increase. The culture has shifted, and it will not return to the way it was. So the responsibility for educational changes falls on the shoulders of schools more now than in the past. These socio-economic shifts in our culture are creating a large amount of stress on teachers and school systems. However, with cluster-grouped classrooms infused with Indigenous learning principles, the transformation of 2e education can happen without undue stress on public-school systems and teachers.

A couple of years ago, FCDS had an all-school reunion at the Morgan Mansion in Los Altos Hills, CA, the prior home of Ford Country Day School. The owner opened the grand estate to allow us to assemble, share stories, reconnect, and remember this extraordinary place. Not long after Brent lost the school, it closed and he died young, a broken heart his wife said. When I discovered he had died, I felt a profound sense of loss as he was one of the most important people in my life.

Brent's wife, Judy, was at the reunion; she almost did not come because of so much hurt over the loss of the school and Brent. It was extraordinary to see her again. It was healing for many of the past students including me. I consider the education received at FCDS to have been excellent and realize this part of my life would have been unnecessary had I experienced an Indigenous learning environment in the school system where I grew up. I also would not have lost all my childhood friends. I have never been able to replace that loss. Yet the FCDS experience was one of the most positive experiences in my life. Something as simple as changing the framing of how teachers deliver education has a profound impact on children's futures. I might have done so much more in my education rather than have my potential squandered as happens to so many 2e children. I have learned and I have persevered and adapted, and my life experience has brought me to this research. Although I did not choose this path, I am the result of my experiences and I am blessed having gone through them.

I use my time at FCDS as a reference point in my life. I feel all children deserve to feel protected, accepted, and nurtured. As I have made life decisions, I am continually trying to find somewhere I can again belong as I did at FCDS. Someplace where I am just fine as I am. Someplace where I do not have to prove my worth day after day, week after week, month after month, and year after year. I ache to work and learn somewhere I am accepted for being me. I often wonder if I am the only one feeling this way but in the back of my mind, I know other children who grow up 2e feel the same way. Knowing this drives me to address the social injustice felt by so many children through the work I did on this book.

Educators have the resources and information necessary to eliminate the injustice but do not necessarily have the mindset to do so. My mission is to transform educator mindsets so every child, 2e or not, can grow up feeling protected, accepted, and nurtured. Creating conversations at the borderlands between those with differing worldviews will be the key to help transform these mindsets, a dialogic and system-based approach not one based on experts dictating solutions. Indigenous learning principles would have helped me with the transition, particularly the infusion of spiritual ecology into the learning setting. Spiritual ecology would have provided me with a stable center for my learning and helped me understand my place in the world, first with my family, then the community, nation, and the world. Through spiritual ecology, I, like other 2e children, would have felt like a valuable part of the world, not lost and separated. If this connection with everything around me had been created early in my school experience, it would have provided a reason for being in this world and the healing and connection I needed to thrive and realize my potential.

My parents also provided me with another critical learning experience matching both my passion for nature and my passion for animals during the time I was at FCDS. In the summers of 1964, 1965, and 1966, my parents arranged for me to attend a month-long summer camp in Northern California. Plantation was a working farm camp located in the middle of the beautiful Northern California redwood forest set above the ocean. Abe and Eve

Crittenden founded the camp and this opportunity proved to be one of the extraordinary experiences of my life. To help defray the costs,

Figure 7.3 Plantation Camp, CA where John Inman spent three summers.

both my parents helped at the camp at one time or another. As a 2e child, I thrived outside of the classroom as many 2e children do. I particularly thrived when in nature and with animals. The camp was divided into small age and gender-specific communities. We lived in tents, had farm chores twice per day, and a wealth of activities to engage an active child like me. Swimming, canoeing, archery, rowing, fort making, hiking, horseback riding, cricket, splitting firewood, and pottery making (we dug our clay) were all ways for me to learn through experience. I excelled in everything I did outside of the classroom setting. Although I thrived in every experience, nothing could compare with my love of the horses. I was on horse chore every time I could select this experience and bonding with these beautiful spirits was one of the highlights of my life.

Nature and this experiential community were my teachers. I gained a spiritual connection with the world around me and I felt part of a community dedicated to my learning. We told stories and myths around the campfire every night igniting my imagination. I was in deep rapport with what I was learning. I dreamed of a life fully connected to nature and animals. I gained a profound connection and understanding of the delicate balance of the world around me. And I had a chance to create art, sing, and dance with friends and mentors. I can imagine few experiences where all Indigenous learning foundations would have been more fully

Figure 7.4 John Inman (middle right) at Plantation Camp.

present. The Plantation experience over those three summers had a lasting impact on how I view the world and view my role in the world. It was also the reason I eventually would earn a degree in Animal Science Pre/Vet Medicine.

When I look back on my recollections, I notice I do not include any specific friends in my conversation. I have lost touch with almost all my friends from FCDS and remember no one from Plantation other than my counselors one year and Abe and Eve. With FCDS, my most vivid memories are of relationships with friends set in the context of what we did together at the school. I remember Brent but I have almost no recollection of any of my teachers. I certainly do not remember how the classes felt or the relationships with the teachers. With Plantation, all my recollections are of experiences, not of people. I can easily run tapes in my mind of everything I was engaged in at Plantation even after 55 years. I am not surprised experiences drive my learning.

Families are so busy now compared with when I grew up. In the current culture, families rush from one event to another. Sports, music, arts, and other activities are all packed into after-school time and weekends. But my childhood culture does not represent how most families live their lives. When I grew up there was far less of this type of over scheduling of time. We went outside and played with friends, and most other activities were through clubs, sports, scouts, and other organizations. I also worked mowing lawns, delivering papers, selling candy, and other endeavors. It seems to me families have fewer opportunities to allow their children to play and grow through less structured activities like those I was able to do as a child. Twice-exceptional children need out of school learning to grow and learn. With the current culture of less unstructured learning for children, schools have even more responsibility to create engaging in-school learning opportunities for 2e children. Just because typical activities I might envision for my children are available to them, it cannot be assumed these experiences are available to most 2e children. This social injustice must be addressed.

Minority 2e children and 2e girls are two groups largely ignored in our school systems. I feel a sense of duty to reach out and help these children along with other 2e and alternative learning children.

Based on my memories growing up and living as a 2e person, I can understand what these children are going through and help them understand their experience. I can also help design learning environments where these children will thrive.

Chapter 8
High School

My time at FCDS also set me up for another life opportunity helping me prepare for college. My brother was a diplomat. Although my parents never had much money, having a brother who worked overseas gave me the chance to visit him and experience other cultures. I visited him in Venezuela, Japan, and Mexico. Engaging with other cultures early in life has contributed to my passion for different ways of knowing and learning. I learned early Western ways of knowing the world were but one perspective and not at all the only acceptable way to experience the world. One of those experiences was traveling to Japan to live with my brother for a year in ninth-grade.

After I left FCDS, I traveled by freighter to Japan with my mother to visit my brother's family. My father had flown to Thailand to do seismograph work to detect troop movements for the government during the Vietnam War as part of his job at Stanford Research Institute (SRI) and would join us for a visit later. My mother stayed a short while and then returned home with my father leaving me to live with my brother's family. As my brother was 19 years older, his children are close in age to me, so I had a whole family with siblings, which was new to me. I did not know them well and had to learn what it was like to live with other children.

I started school in Tokyo at Nishimachi International School in September with my nephews and niece. I was in a small ninth-grade class with all girls and one other boy, the son of the Czechoslovakian ambassador to Japan. Zadaniak was my best friend and very interesting.

Zadaniak was a diehard Communist, spoke Czech, Russian, English, Japanese, Chinese, and was proficient in other romance languages. He changed his political opinions I found out later after standing in the square in his hometown watching the Russian army invade his homeland. Zadaniak was worldly and I was just a

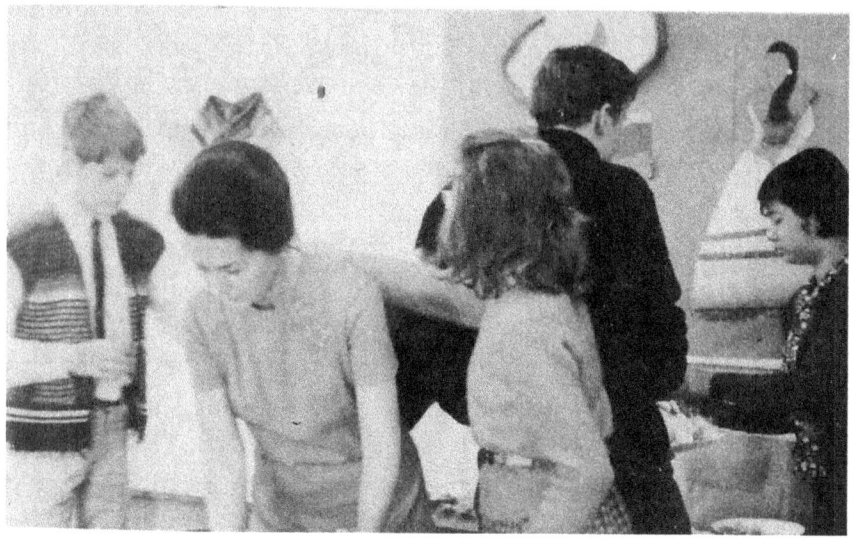

Figure 8.1 Nishimachi school, Tokyo Japan ninth-grade class (John Inman on left).

middle-class, politically naive American kid who struggled with English. He was a bit daunting for me and anything but politically naive, but since I went to school with very wealthy kids for four years at FCDS, he just seemed like another kid to me. He played the accordion and I was attempting to play the guitar and we would sit for hours and play and sing together. School in Tokyo was grueling. I did OK but flunked Japanese. I would have been completely lost if I have not just finished four years at FCDS. My experience in Tokyo was amazing. My nephews and I would go out and explore Tokyo regularly. We lived near the Olympic stadium and swam there in the summer and ice skated there in the winter. We took the train to Yokohama every week for Boy Scouts, an experience I will never forget. But unfortunately, my stay was cut short. My father was born with a deformed aorta valve and was called into emergency surgery in January for open-heart surgery. I left Tokyo for home and my father's surgery never to return to Japan.

The international school and FCDS experiences were similar in many respects. Both had small classes and dedicated teachers were the norm. The students were certainly well above average and both were performance environments. Nishimachi International School was fun but very intense. Although an international school with the classes taught in English, it was still situated in Tokyo, a culture far different than the culture I grew up in. What I learned most while living in Tokyo was an interest in the culture. Being in a new culture created an experience where the world around me became my learning lab. The learning environment was far more structured than at FCDS. There was very little adaptation to different learning styles and there was more of an expert-based style of teaching. I found this setting challenging and adapting was difficult. My activities outside of the classroom certainly related more to Indigenous learning than the experience inside of the classroom. With the multiple nationalities in the school, a more nuanced educational approach probably would have been beneficial.

When I came back home from Tokyo, I started back to public-school to finish my ninth-grade year at Jordan Junior High School in Palo Alto, CA. Although I knew no one, I felt more engaged at Jordan than any other time after my experiences at FCDS and Nishimachi. I learned to drive, learned to type, was on the debate team, and the board diving team. Although I was only in Jordan for half a year, I did well there. I do not remember anything about the classes I took, but I do not have negative memories of my time there.

My learning journey over the five years from fifth-grade through ninth-grade taught me the skills I needed to learn and read and gave me a sense of how I could interact with the world. These were invaluable experiences; without which I am convinced I would not have completed my doctorate. I suspect those who have not experienced growing up 2e might disbelieve I have challenges as a learner. After all, I have earned two bachelor's degrees, two master's degrees, and my doctorate. I believe my efforts to earn degrees is my way to prove to myself I am not as dumb as I felt growing up.

The pervasive harm to my sense of efficacy and self-esteem, the effects of which challenge me to this day, cannot be seen. Others cannot see or feel the impact of what it is like growing up 2e, but the damage has had a profound impact on my life and how I have or have not been able to realize my potential and contribute to the world. Western culture struggles to recognize the impact on an alternative learning child not fitting the norm without visible demonstration that damage exists. When children act out in classrooms, are hyperactive, daydream, or struggle with assignments, there very well might be underlying learning difficulties or gifts ignored. In an Indigenous learning environment, waiting to see the damage would not be the preferred strategy. The culture would instead be more concerned with process and experience and act from this cultural framework. In application, integrating these strategies would provide scaffolding supporting 2e children to grow and develop their gifts, rather than wait and see if they struggle with a more mechanistic approach.

When I started high school, I took with me the skills for learning and reading I had learned over the prior 5 years and I also took with me a lack of self-efficacy and self-esteem developed during my first 6 years of school. Unfortunately, the latter dominated my high school experience. I did not like high school. I went to school and went home and then went to work. With two exceptions, geology and chemistry, the years I spent at Palo Alto High School are so unmemorable, I remember little of the experience. I was lonely and did not fit in. I did not know anyone and was a quiet kid. My focus was on trying to survive, not to thrive. I was bored and the classes were not compelling. I certainly did not feel connected to the school, the curriculum, the teachers, or the other students. I worked hard to finish a half year early so I could leave. I did not go to the graduation ceremony. I cannot imagine feeling more disconnected from the world around me during this time in my school life.

My high school years were a time when I was highly suspicious of any attempt to convince me of "the" right way of knowing. The introduction of multiple histories through Indigenizing the curriculum would have had a transformative impact on my high school experience. As a 2e child, I saw complexity where simple solutions were taught, and I did not buy into what was offered as truth. This was true for me in religion as well as education. I reeled against what I saw as the hypocrisy of formal religion. Where was social justice and compassion? I resented being told only one path to the Creator existed. How could the Creator provide so many experiences when only one path was approved? I walked away from religion for over 20 years and when I returned, I would not accept any message of intolerance. I could see nothing but complexity and could not understand how others saw only simple solutions. I felt the same way about history in high school. How could only one perspective be representative of reality? It was not for me. I saw the complexity of history and accepted no simple explanation. If my high school curriculum were Indigenized, I would have been engaged and fascinated with history; instead, I was confronted with facts which were not facts and memorization of data. History could not have been less compelling to me. Most of my high school experience would have been greatly enriched had an Indigenized curriculum been the norm.

During high school, as with other times in my education, my most compelling learning experiences were outside of the classroom. Camping and being outdoors kept me grounded during these years. As I loved being outdoors and away from the city, I often considered what it might have been like to grow up in an Indigenous culture, one far more integrated into the natural world. When away from school and the classroom, I was creative and innovative. I excelled at so many things, all of which would have been integral to a more experiential and dialogic education setting, one Indigenous learning strategies would have created. For the most part, except for geology and chemistry, classes in high school were lectures on stuff to which I simply did not relate. If these topics were connected to real-world issues, if the curriculum had been designed to build on my strengths as a 2e learner, I would have had an entirely different experience. It might have been a high school experience that set me up for a life and career based on confidence and belief in myself rather than reinforcing childhood patterns of self-doubt and demoralization about my ability to learn and fit in. I have tried to imagine what I would have gained had I been spiritually connected to what I was supposed to learn. I would have felt a part of the learning community, would have been able to use stories and myth to envision a world I wanted to live in, my education would have honored integration with the world, and my dialogic capabilities leveraged. All of this would have been created within an Indigenous learning context and would have transformed my high school experience.

My family camped. I grew up outdoors. My father was a desert rat and was fondly decorated as a royal radiated desert rat as all his SRI team members worked in Nevada doing the seismograph work for government nuclear tests. My father loved camping in the desert and being outdoors as much as he could manage. I grew to love the desert and being outdoors as much as my father did. I still love the desert, a passion the rest of my family does not share. We both felt a bond to Indigenous cultures and how they lived with, not on the land. When Dad grew up in the early 1900s in Oklahoma, he invested a substantial amount of time on the Indian Reservation in the region. He loved the Indigenous culture. And this coming from a short redhead who could look no more different than the Indigenous cultures he loved so much. This translated into our outings to scour the desert for pottery, arrowheads, and anything else providing insights into these ancient cultures. Dad taught me how to make arrowheads, arrows, and bows. I still have the materials and tools to do this work. I always loved to create and explore, build, and innovate. I did not have to read, I could use my gifts, gifts I did not know I had. I just knew what I loved to do, and it rarely revolved around schoolwork. My family respected the world around us; we took care to never scar or damage what we

Figure 8.2 My father, Louis Howard Inman, in the field for SRI.

loved so much. I grew up loving nature and living with a deep respect for the world. Yes, we are Western European in origin, but our family grew up with a deep respect for those who came before us, the Indigenous populations. My experience growing up provided me with a passion for learning more about Indigenous cultures and what we could learn from them to protect the world. During my high school years, the more time I was able to allocate hiking, camping, and being outdoors, the happier I was. So graduating early provided me with just a little extra time to do what I loved.

I find it interesting that I have little to say about my high school experience. I have many memories of this time in my life and little of it came from school. I simply do not remember much of the experience, with one exception. I was very lonely. I had but one friend and spent most of my time alone or working. I was terrified of girls as a shy kid and did not socialize at all. Although I am comfortable in conversations at work and about work, when it comes to personal conversations and relationships, I am still quite shy. As a result, my story revolves around my connection with the world around me and again, non-school experiences had far more impact on me as a young man than school ever did.

When talking with others, it seems high school was a fun and engaging time in their lives. High schools include a strong culture of events, dances, dating, sports, and friendships for many, and I missed all this culture when I was in high school. How many other children experience this level of disconnection with their high school experience? I suspect other 2e children who struggle with meaning in high school might experience something similar. I wonder if high school administrative cultures would be willing to explore modifying the system to create a more meaningful experience for 2e and other alternative learning children. To do so will require letting go of the expert model of knowledge and engaging with others across borders of perspective in dialogue to co-create new paths forward, paths unable to be created with only singular perspectives.

Chapter 9
My Undergraduate College Years

After high school, I worked full time to earn money for college and camped and hiked until I left for college. I had January through August to engage with the world around me before stepping back into a school setting. Once I selected a college, Oregon State University, I focused on the transition. I was raised to be independent, a self-thinker, and self-reliant. Living away from home was one thing but believing I could go to college and be successful was quite another.

My public-school experiences were daunting without the support and encouragement provided at FCDS. My parents knew how hard school was for me and just hoped I would try college, but they did not understand the depth of my persistence in the face of adversity. If nothing else, growing up 2e steeled me for the knocks I faced, and I have faced repeatedly as I have developed through life. They never understood just what it took to compensate for my learning deficit, but they soon found out just how hard I was willing to work to achieve my goals.

I started to college in geological oceanography wanting to follow in my father's footsteps and learn a geological science. I loved the ocean and scuba dove during high school with my friend from FCDS, Steven Koch. I also loved geology and hunting for rocks and understanding the origin of the rock formations I grew up exploring. My father was a geophysicist, brilliant in mathematics and electrical engineering, as well. So, although I thought I wanted to follow in my father's footsteps and do something around the geological sciences, I certainly was not prepared for the work to set me up for success in math and science-intensive fields of study. I was no match for the math and science classes and just about flunked out during the first year. I dropped out for a year and worked to get in-state tuition in Oregon as my parents were not able to help me financially after the first year. I then came back in Animal Science/Pre-Vet medicine with the hope of becoming a vet.

Reading was still very difficult for me as I started back to college. I felt I had to do something to help me survive this time around. When I came back to school after working a year, I decided to take a speed-reading course to help with my reading. As I listened to other participants and observed their progress, it was clear to me I simply was unable to do what they could do. This was discouraging but I did improve and was grateful for the improvement even though I never got the results others seemed to get. My college experience would have been even more difficult than it was if I had not taken the initiative to improve my reading. Over the next four years, I worked and went to school 16 terms straight without a break so I could complete degrees in Animal Science and Business Management.

The speed-reading course did not solve my learning problems. The science-intensive Animal Science/Pre-Vet Medicine program challenged me, but I loved the subject and worked hard to learn the field. Through pure hard work and persistence, I did complete the program but not with grades allowing me to get into vet school. I felt lost in being unable to pursue what I loved, working with animals. As a 2e child, I was drawn to animals as they provided unconditional love and expected nothing of me but caring and respect in return. Over the years, horses and dogs have been some of my very best friends. Especially being without a dog leaves a large gap in my heart.

As a 2e person, I am very good with patterns and so much so in genetics, my genetics professor wanted me to stay and pursue a doctorate with him. I was flattered but had absolutely no confidence in my ability to do such work and passed by the opportunity. If my first six years of school had nurtured my gifts and helped me mitigate my dyslexia, this roadblock would not have existed. I can only imagine how many 2e children never get the chance to realize their potential because of similar experiences.

As a part of my coursework to earn my Agriculture (Ag) degree, I was required to take an Ag Business Management course and

Figure 9.1 John Inman with an Airedale Terrier puppy, his favorite breed.

found I had a keen understanding of organizations and how people organize and decided to pursue a management degree in addition to my Animal Science degree, graduating with dual degrees. I never missed classes because I had to hear the lectures to get the material. I made it through both degrees with a discipline I have brought to my work, a discipline necessary for me to survive. I bring this same discipline to my passion for education.

I have always felt a sense of connection to the world when away from modern society. I do not hunt or fish for recreation like so many others who enjoy the outdoors, rather I like to simply experience and connect with this extraordinary natural world. I have never lost my wonder of creation and feel blessed every day I can live to experience the world. Connecting with the natural world provides a spiritual experience for me and has always been a source of strength as I have traveled life's journey. The spirituality sustains me and helps me thrive in a Western world where things are more important than the relationship with the world we live in. Educators could infuse this sense of spirituality into Western education through the addition of Indigenous learning principles. I wonder how healing a spiritual connection with the world would be for other 2e children as it was for me.

My story does not represent the vast learning experience I had in college, but it does capture my sense of who I was and what I was to become. My first-year failure was difficult and my inability to progress to vet school was also difficult and my writing reflects this. As I think about why my story emerged this way, I am struck with an unexplored open wound, the fact I have been unable to invest in a career working with animals. I have tried to work in the pet industry and in an Ag co-op but just did not find a good fit. I probably would have thrived as a wildlife biologist. My story introduced me to my sense of loss of this career. I endeavor to look forward and not look to past losses, but this has been a tough life lesson. I am hoping to volunteer in a wildlife refuge when I retire so that I can get back to working with animals.

I am struck with the lack of mentorship in Western culture. There are mentors but few children and adults have access to mentors. Ideally, both k-12 and college teachers would be listening and looking for strengths and gifts and help students with choices. This rarely happened for me except with my genetics professor. And on the flip side, I was not very good at asking for help: I was independent. This did not help me on my quest and has ended up a roadblock many times in my life. If we had teachers who viewed their roles as mentors and guides rather than simply being subject matter experts, 2e children would have a much better chance to find and realize their gifts. To do this, teachers would have to embrace a dialogic approach and the rich collection of ways to know the world. It would then be easy for teachers to hear what children are trying to say through their actions and words.

My learning experiences as a 2e child and adult have helped me become passionate about how to treat both children and adults. I focus my thinking on dialogic practices and the emergence of knowledge through dialogue. My work is focused on treating people with respect, regardless of their age or background, and through doing so helping develop people into their potential. This has turned out to be my mission in life.

Chapter 10
The Journey to My First Master's Degree

The Impact of Living as a 2e Person

Patterns I learned in k-5 as a 2e child have repeated throughout my life. Unfortunately, many of these patterns have been unhealthy; they have been patterns I learned to help protect me from a world viewing me as broken and not fulfilling my potential. I would have learned to interface with the world differently within an Indigenous environment. Twice-exceptional children expend so much energy trying to guard, defend, protect, and maintain, they have little energy left to realize their potential. Educators often fail to grasp the extent of this social injustice in schools and their inaction exasperates the problem, leaving hundreds of thousands of 2e children without the support they need. My experience has been no different. The amount of work invested to try to break these life patterns has been daunting. The way I have learned to interface with the world not only has framed my work and personal life, but the patterns also followed me to my first master's degree in education. I started my master's degree in adult education in September of 2000, just as the dot com crash started.

Why I Chose to Earn a Master's in Adult Education

As I sat wondering if my dreams would be dashed, my gut twisted as the director of the program indicated the graduate school of education at Oregon State University did not believe I was capable of graduate work and I would be put on probation to enter the master's degree program. I felt I needed to pour out my heart in my application to overcompensate for what would be the result of a new effort; they would think I was broken. I was reliving a story I had been living my whole life, one of being learning-disabled. This was in 2000, long before I understood I had gifts as well as learning deficits. But here was my new graduate professor who brought another message. I listened to his words and his heart and he believed in me. He had written a letter to the graduate committee asking that I be given a chance. He felt I would be a value to his cohort. I felt lightheaded but almost grim as I reflected on what this meant. Was what he was saying true or was I perceiving something that did not exist? Was I just making it up?

Although I was plagued with doubt as I joined my new cohort members for orientation in a non-air-conditioned room in the ancient building housing the graduate school of education at Oregon State University, I was also filled with hope. I could not help but feel I was an imposter. Maybe the admissions board was right. I looked around the room and I wondered if I belonged with this talented group of professionals all with robust backgrounds in adult education. Or were they just as scared as I was? I had none of their educational backgrounds. I felt humbled. But I knew I wanted to change course in my career, to get away from the high stress of being in business development and follow my heart to help others realize their potential.

As I think back, my gift of perseverance helped me through my master's degree program. I had also deliberately chosen a program fitting my learning style. The program was project-based and founded on a learner-centered, outcome-based framework. We met as a cohort once per month and the rest of the work was project-based. Without knowing it, I chose a program honoring Indigenous learning as the program honored different gifts and paths, was dialogic and experiential, system inspired, and was founded on a learning community format. I would not have done well in a traditional linear classroom setting. Most programs are still expert programs based on lectures and 2e children are most likely to end up in such a program. I did make it through my undergraduate education in this format, but it was extremely difficult. Like other 2e students, I would have done far better in a dialogic and collaborative learning environment, one modeled by Indigenous learning principles.

It had taken me 7 years to make this step, one I had envisioned while I was attempting to make my way in the world as an organizational consultant. It was 1991 and the Persian Gulf War had just started, and I had been working leading a team of 23 construction sales consultants for a large remodeling business in Portland. This was yet again another position in a long string of positions where I did not feel at home. It was not my place, but I had work to support my family. I felt as I always did as I started over, I had to prove myself. I built good relationships and was able to provide good leadership for this team, but in the end, it did not matter as my position was eliminated when the construction contracts in the market dried up because of the Persian Gulf War. This was one of many transitions in my life; I wondered what to do.

After talking it over with my wife, I decided to strike out on my own and start a consulting firm. After all, if I could run and build businesses, certainly I could help others do the same. Even though I have never jumped out of a plane with a parachute, starting my consulting practice in Portland with no independent consulting background felt like my own personal parachute jump. A friend said he would provide a contract half time to help me get started. My work with him lasted a couple of months and then I was on my own.

I am quite sure I have never worked so hard for so little. I loved the creativity, the learning, the helping of teams grow and become healthy, but working alone and asking for payment for services was difficult. I continuously questioned if I had anything to offer. My lack of self-efficacy and self-esteem were an ever-present part of me. Could I even add value, I wondered? Doubt about who I was and what I had to offer plagued me as I continued down this path. Doubt has been a reoccurring pattern throughout my life. If I had grown up in an educational environment where my gifts were honored, where I felt a connection with my learning, where I felt I had a place in the world, all outcomes from the infusion of Indigenous learning, this reoccurring pattern would not have existed. I consider the impact on Western culture from children growing up into adults who lack confidence, to be a solvable problem if we alter the mindsets of educators to embrace cluster-grouped classrooms and Indigenous learning principles. Borderland conversations between those with an Indigenous worldview and those with a Western worldview will be the key in creating the context for the co-creation of new pathways, an integral part of my recommendations.

It felt to me like I had to work harder with fewer rewards growing up 2e than others. I also had an unsettled feeling of not belonging. This was the case as I started my consulting work. I wanted to be accepted and I wanted to help.

Figure 10.1 John Inman at the radio station in Portland, OR.

As I worked doing many different things to try to keep my consulting business afloat, one of the most creative strategies to get better known in the market was a radio talk show I created at the small business radio station in Portland Oregon (see Figure 10.1). I interviewed leading figures in the region whose knowledge would be helpful to me and others. One of those people was Larry Wilson of Pecos River Learning Centers. Larry, who had founded Wilson Learning, was a mentor even though I had never met him. When I had experienced counselor salesperson training from Wilson Learning in 1983, I finally found it was OK to be ethical and honest and be able to be a professional consultant in sales, the field I had fallen into just a few years before.

Larry had agreed to allow me to interview him for my show after a couple of months of negotiation with his assistant. If I am nothing else, I am persistent, and it was this persistence that convinced Larry to let me interview him. After the interview, I hesitated and then mustered the courage to ask my final question; I asked Larry if he saw a way I might work with him. He invited me to New Mexico to Pecos River Learning to experience his work and to meet him. I could not believe it. He had said yes, at least to a conversation. It was 1993 and my consulting was running thin and here was an opportunity to meet Larry Wilson and possibly work with him. I jumped at the chance.

I had invested hundreds of hours listening to Larry's audiotapes, reading his books, studying his materials, and applying his principles over the prior 11 years. Although I was not generally confident, I was confident I was an expert on counselor selling and the consulting process Larry taught. I was also excited to participate in his work at Pecos, which was experientially-based change leadership, a field of practice I loved. I felt a strong bond with this work as it was experiential and fit my learning style perfectly. His work could have been inspired by Indigenous learning principles as it focused on team, experience, dialogue, and, given the learning center was in the middle of ancient Indigenous lands, it might have been Indigenous-inspired. I arranged to fly down to New Mexico. After the long bus ride to the learning center and after I had checked into my room, I ventured over to a session where Larry was talking. What an uncanny experience to stand and hear and see Larry talk.

When he was finished with the session, he came over, and I introduced myself. As we talked, I felt as though I was talking to myself. I had integrated so much of Larry into me it was uncanny.

This work was part of me, part of my language, and part of my worldview. I was emotionally connected to this work and this man. This was work I wanted to do, people I wanted to work with, and a

Figure 10.2 John Inman and Larry Wilson at Pecos River Learning in New Mexico.

place I felt at home. Having Larry's extensive body of work on tape allowed me to listen, learn, and absorb material I would have been unable to fully integrate through a typical Western lecture format. It was oral learning, a framework I thrived in, and one honoring Indigenous oral tradition. I could imagine sitting in a circle listening to Larry's stories. His messages were always delivered through stories. I had not realized how aligned Larry's work was to my learning style and my view of the world around me.

After a couple of trips down to New Mexico to work with Larry, my time with him was complete. As I was getting ready to leave to head back to Portland, Larry and I were talking on the patio and I asked him again if he could see a way I might work with him. He did not even miss a heartbeat and simply said no. I did not have the background or the credentials to work with him. I was heartbroken. It was at that moment I understood what I must do, I needed to go back to school and earn an advanced degree to build my credentials. Although I was deflated and hurt, I understood I had tried to play in a game for which I was not prepared. I would just go out and prove I could do this work, whatever this work was. My ability to quickly understand and synthesize disparate inputs has helped me reposition my career many times. Each time I repositioned was time I might have invested gaining mastery in a field rather than spent learning a new field. I wonder how many adults who grew up 2e have developed patterns like mine. It has been a long journey to learn to overcome these patterns when all this time I could have been investing in fulfilling my potential. Instead of suffering the large loss of social capital from underdeveloped 2e children and adults, we could be using this social capital to help solve real-world problems. We have the chance to break this cycle and make sure 2e children have the chance to realize their potential if we start to make the right decisions. Those decisions include integrating cluster grouping strategies into schools and adding Indigenous learning strategies into classrooms. The transformation to an integrated educational model starts with abandoning solutions based only on expert models that do not represent new knowledge born out of dialogue at the borderlands between differing worldviews.

Consulting Coming to an End

My career as an independent consultant was coming to an end and I had virtually abandoned my wife and young son as I worked ridiculous hours trying to do the work I needed to do to support them. Yet I was not making the income needed to sustain my family. My friend who had helped me with some work as I started my consulting practice had a small three-person software startup and he asked me to join him to help build his company. He was the consummate businessperson, an MBA, and epitomized an entrepreneur. I was not from his industry, telecommunications, and for the several years I worked with him and his partner, I struggled to prove the value I added. I was instrumental in building his business and I made the partners a lot of money, yet I never felt a part of the club.

My friend did not understand how I thought. I was so unlike him. I looked at the world differently. In conversations, he would wonder aloud how to best utilize me. I delivered unmistakable value, but I did not look and act like others in business, so the value was questioned. As I think differently, I always seemed odd to them. I have never quite figured out how to deal with this. If I had learned my gifts early in my education, I suspect my struggle would have ended much earlier or never started. An Indigenous learning environment would have provided me with what I needed to discover my gifts. He knew I could connect to our clients better than anyone he had ever worked with, yet he would end up trusting those who were more like him. To this day he will tell me his firm would have failed if it had not been for me. I saved and built his business, but I do not think he ever understood how I did so.

I felt out of place growing up being unable to learn the way others learned, being unable to memorize like others did, having a passion for justice, and having a worldview not matching others in the business world. It was no different working with my friend at the software startup. I liked the people and I tried to fit in, but in my heart, I never felt like I fit. I felt a deep sense of insecurity with who I was. Who was I if I did not fit anywhere I went? Who would I become, I thought? I tried many things, and nothing felt like it fit with who I was. Even now I wonder if I had only been told about being a wildlife biologist in college, I would have chosen a different path. It was with this deep sense of dis-ease I finally found my way to the graduate school of education at Oregon State University. It took 6 years working with the software startup before I felt I could afford to pursue my master's degree after Larry told me I had no credentials. I finally got to the point where I could make this decision and started another leg of my journey to become a respected contributor to the world and left the software firm for college. The anticipated hard work for the master's degree in adult education did not concern me as hard work helps me compensate and look competent to those around me and has also provided the foundation for success in each endeavor I have chosen.

To fit in, I work hard to develop my competence. I feel others will accept me if I look and act competent and I work a bit harder than others to get to this state. In my master's degree program it always amazed me how everyone knew the theorists and could speak to each and their work as if it were second nature. I struggled just to learn who these theorists were. The language never came easily to me.

I am a change agent by nature and when I start over, I often create the very roadblocks I am trying to overcome. It is hard to show competence if you change your career every 3 years. The neverending quest to fit in has driven my decisions and actions, an unnecessary quest if I had grown up with my gifts honored and developed. I ask myself if this is just an excuse for not being smart or am I just being lazy as I was told as I grew up. I like me but why do I have to struggle so hard? Why do I make things so hard on myself and my family? As I wrote my doctoral dissertation, I wondered if I would be able to help others who struggle as I have. I was not sure. I wondered who would care about what I had to offer. I was different, with a different perspective, and I wondered how this would play out. My legacy from early Western education manifests in this nagging thought pattern. I would have welcomed being treated like I had valuable gifts in an Indigenous learning environment. I still would have lived with challenges, I am human after all, but I would have lived without the pervasive doubts born from being treated as if I had no value.

Feelings of inadequacy, feelings of being unaccepted, feelings of being isolated, and feelings of being unable to contribute well up from my childhood experience as a 2e child. This psychic wound has followed me throughout my life. I have relived this story many times. I have invested thousands of hours of work to heal myself and have made great progress, but the underlying experience of what has created me as a human never goes away. I can mitigate its impact through my efforts, but my reactions and my decisions still flow out of my experience as a 2e person trying to make his way in a Western positivist culture not honoring different ways of knowing and being. Only through my persistence am I able to continue forward. My experience growing up and living as a 2e person and investing thousands of hours trying to figure out how to fit in the Western world provided a clear picture of the social injustice of poor learning environments for 2e children. Multiplying this experience by hundreds of thousands of children and then adding the time invested by 2e children trying to survive rather than realizing their gifts illustrates the magnitude of the impact. Adding Indigenous learning principles situated in cluster-grouped classrooms provides an easy and powerful solution to turn this travesty around and would have transformed my educational experience growing up.

Chapter 11
Overcoming Barriers to Dialogue

I have experienced and witnessed the roadblocks to dialogue and collaboration in the Western educational paradigm and how these roadblocks might have been reduced or eliminated using Indigenous and dialogic frameworks. To make an impact and create opportunities for 2e children and other children with alternative learning capabilities, educators should explore using a targeted approach with cluster grouping strategies combined with Indigenous principles. This framework would have provided me with a learning environment where I would have thrived.

Although my k-5 experience excluded these principles, my 5-8 experience began to integrate some of these principles. Principles included a cluster-grouped classroom with teachers able to address a variety of learning capabilities in one classroom and integrating into the curriculum multimodalities such as those found in an Indigenous framework. However, I do not believe a child should have to be placed in a private school or an alternative school to experience these strategies. As a social justice issue, 2e children in all schools should have this opportunity. 2e children can experience a transformation if the learning environment design supports the change. My learning environment did not fully support change, so transformation was difficult. To provide for my transformation, I first needed to transform myself and overcome the barriers to my journey. Barriers to dialogue are both self-imposed by 2e children and are systemic. Both must be addressed to transform education systems. I have addressed both internal and exterior barriers to transform my ability to learn.

Internal Barriers to Dialogue

I am beginning to overcome the story of being learning-disabled. As I grew up believing I had no gifts, the LD label framed my identity. I have found abandoning this story difficult as I have lived the story my whole life. Yet I am shifting to a new story. It has taken a lot of work, but I now live the story of growing up 2e and embracing the gifts 2e has provided. I no longer consider myself learning-disabled. Yet I embrace learning differently, knowing differently, and having a different way of seeing the world as well as having gifts making me an extraordinary person. I hope educators will step up and help 2e children create new stories to live into and do so before these 2e children live substantial portions of their lives without knowing their gifts. I believe headway can be made to have this vision made real for the thousands of children who need hope in their lives. My dream is to contribute in some small way through my story and foster conversations between worldviews to co-create a new future non-envisioned by those currently in the system.

Children who grow up 2e, as I did, do not know they need a learning environment based on dialogue. They are not schooled in learning theory; they just know they are struggling or failing in the authoritative classroom environment. If these children were to understand this was what they needed, they could self-direct their experience by asking for dialogic learning environments. As they cannot do this, educators must create a dialogic setting for children, not expect children to explain the need for a dialogic setting. I was 60 years old when I discovered my decisions throughout my career drew me to dialogic settings and practices. I did not understand I was doing this. I was acting out of instinct. Educators cannot expect hundreds of thousands of 2e children to self-discover what they need to thrive in the world. I happen to be one of the 2e people who is driven by education and self-discovery and even with thousands of hours of work, it took me 55 years to figure out I thrived only in dialogic settings. If not introduced and educated in dialogic practices, 2e children can be crippled in their ability to self-discover and overcome their learning deficits. To ensure I could thrive in my doctoral program I took a variety of steps. The steps I took might seem extreme to people who are not 2e, but they were necessary for me.

Before I started my doctoral journey at Fielding Graduate University, I took two steps to help me prepare so I would be able to thrive in this rigorous environment. I knew I needed a new story to live into but with near 50 years of living the story of being learning-disabled and broken, I had to do something to make a profound change in my story or it simply would not seem real. My son had given me the book *The Brain That Changes Itself* (Doidge, 2007) the Christmas of 2007 and in reading it, a whole new world opened to me. I discovered the concept of a plastic brain able to change. The concept of neuroplasticity changed my perspective on my learning disability. I discovered I might be able to remap my brain to help overcome my deficit. I did extensive research on neuroplasticity and even contacted Dr. Merzenich, one of the leading researchers in the world, and sought out his insights into how to remap my brain. With the advice of Dr. Merzenich, I purchased the Posit Science program *The Brain Fitness Program* and invested 40 hours of intensive brain exercises to improve the function of my brain and hopefully remap how my brain worked. I made some strong improvements in performance and was encouraged.

The next step I took was to find out if all my learning problems were just a figment of my imagination or were real. I had always believed in the back of my mind maybe I was just not smart. These feelings had haunted me, and I needed to take the risk to find out if this was true. So I started on a new leg of my journey, a leg needing completion before I could create a new story to live into. I needed to find someone who could and would assess a learning-disabled adult and help me discover the answer to my question, Am I learning-disabled?

I found it difficult to find a psychologist willing to assess learning disabilities in an adult. Maybe if I were in San Francisco it would be easy, but in Central Oregon where I was living, it was a challenge. I researched, contacted, and called multiple sources and finally received a referral to a child psychologist who specialized in assessing and working with autistic children in Bend, Oregon who was willing to assess me. She was very kind and open to my quest. I did not have good memories of psychologists from my experiences being assessed as a child. I had lived a lifetime believing I was broken and in need of fixing because of my early experiences. Deciding to go to a psychologist for assessment was quite a leap of faith. Maybe she would confirm my worst fears. Maybe she would not. But I had to know. There was no way I could start a doctoral program believing I was broken. I had to take the risk and be assessed. As I look at this experience from the outside, how odd it seems. Who would do such a thing? The answer to the question would be a 2e person who never was told he had any gifts and who believed he could not learn well.

I had not been in a psychologist's office for 45 years and I was more than a bit nervous. While sitting and waiting, a teen boy was brought into the clinic in shackles by a sheriff. Now there was something I was not used to. Yet it was only another human in need of help, and I relaxed and waited. The doctor came out and we went back to her office and after some questions and an effort to get me to relax we proceeded with the assessment which took several hours. The results did not come until a couple of weeks later, but it was well worth the wait. I went back to her office and met with her and went through the results. She provided graphs and charts and her explanations were excellent. I provided one such graph in the introduction.

If her interaction with me was any indication, I could see why she was so good with children. As it turns out I am in the 98th percentile in intelligence and when adjusted for my dyslexia, would probably be 10 points higher. I am also in about the 45th percentile in reading and spelling, a full three standard deviations below my intelligence. She said this is highly unusual and unexpected with someone who had the education and professional background I had. The results demonstrated I was probably learning-disabled, and I now actually have a legal accommodation for my reading. Wow. I do not use the accommodation as I have learned how to compensate, and I have taken further steps to mitigate my reading disability. But it was wonderful to know I had not made the whole thing up. After decades of wondering, I finally knew, I was not broken, I simply did not read as others did.

There were a couple of outcomes helping me create a new story to live into. First, I was not lying to myself. I do struggle reading and I am not stupid. In fact, I was able to join Mensa. I did so to help me fully believe I was smart, and this was critical to my new story. Never in my life did I ever believe I could be considered smart. I no longer felt broken. This was a huge step for me. This whole series of decisions and actions taken would have been unnecessary if I had grown up with a healthy self-image. With an Indigenous learning framework, I would have grown up believing in myself and my ability to contribute. It amazes me the amount of damage coming from the experience in those first 6 years of school. As I created conversations and did further explorations about the brain and learning disabilities, I discovered something else creating a change in my ability to read.

Through my research, I also learned about a brain sensitivity to light known as Scotopic Sensitivity Syndrome. This sensitivity can contribute to learning disabilities, autism, and many other brain dysfunctions. I have always had a severe sensitivity to light, and I felt compelled to see what this was and whether my sensitivity to light could contribute to my reading problems. The syndrome has been labeled Irlen Syndrome after the educational psychologist Helen Irlen who identified the syndrome in the 1980s. The application of color overlays for reading or custom color prescription glasses provides a solution for Irlen Syndrome. I decided to have a basic evaluation and found when I tried to read black letters on a white page, my brain could not keep a focus on the letters. The result was I could not focus on a page without extreme straining. Reading was exhausting and this syndrome could have been a contributing factor to my lifelong reading struggles. Based on what I learned, I tried overlays, and this helped immensely. Teachers often use these. But as I highlight as I read, it was very awkward moving the overlay page to page. I eventually had a full evaluation and purchased Irlen reading glasses. They are uncovered by insurance and are expensive, but I now cannot imagine doing computer work without them. I no longer become exhausted when I read, and I can easily keep a focus on the page I am reading. This has not eliminated my reading challenges but has made reading easier. As I reflect on the actions I have taken to help me thrive on my learning journey, I return to the story that I lived and my efforts to change that story through these actions, bringing me back to the beginning of my journey.

It was 1962 and by all observable accounts, I was just like any other child in my school. I had friends, I played, I had fun, and I had a loving family. But something was amiss. I was unable to read like other children and the Western education system in Palo Alto, CA did not recognize I was not really like other kids. They thought I was lazy and not as smart and treated me so. I learned early on just because my disability was not visible to others, did not make it not exist. My pain was real. My humiliation was real. My struggles were real. My fears were real. I have lived out this reality creating so many problems in my life. I have not felt I fit in and have not had a sense of place. Is there something wrong with me? Why can I not simply fit in and accept what is around me as others do? Why do I fight so hard to protect my sense of who I am? Why do I flee when I feel I am not accepted? Why do I get so angry if someone does not trust me or questions my integrity? I no longer think I am broken and in need of fixing even though I have lived a lifetime thinking this. I now see a pattern that can be traced back to my early childhood experience of growing up 2e. I have relived this pattern repeatedly throughout my life. I can now clearly see the story I was living into. This story was creating the experience of the life I was living. I also now realize I can live into a new story.

I have written my new story. I am not easily living into this story. I still fight to be accepted, get angry, get discouraged, and question who I am, but my new story guides my growth into the person I envision: a person in communication with the universe; a loving and compassionate person; a smart and capable person; a person who loves the different ways of knowing of all people, human and non-human; a person who wants to contribute to this world; and, a person willing to work to make a difference in the lives of others. I am this person who I brought to my doctoral work. This person engages fully in the transformation of the world and hopes in turn for acceptance from the world. I have hope and passion for the story I am living into. Growing up 2e will always be a part of who I am and what I bring to this world; it just no longer controls who I hope to become. I can create a sense of place for myself outside of my household. I am excited to find a community where I feel at home, I am excited to find a community of practice where I can contribute, I am excited to understand the deep dialogic nature of my learning style, and I look to the mountain to guide my journey. In this journey, I have found completion and a deep connection with the world. I am home.

External Barriers to Dialogue

We are a deliberative culture in the Western world, particularly in the US, not a dialogic culture. We like to discuss things, tear them apart, fix things (people), and make decisions. One can hear the reverberations throughout organization halls, we do not have time to talk, and we must get things done. Then add to this the history of expert-based knowledge transfer in Western culture and dialogue almost disappears. Collaborative strategies are certainly the rage; however, implementing dialogic strategies within a dualistic mindset creates challenges. Educators can go through the steps but will quickly revert to an expert model if they still are steeped in Western ways of knowing. Educators will still want to direct, control, and tell unless they accept a fundamental shift in mindset. Bringing Indigenous learning principles to the classroom and Indigenizing the classroom through the introduction of alternative histories can have a profound impact on changing mindsets to counter the dualistic worldview.

I have experienced the attempt to use dialogic strategies situated in dualistic settings over and over again as I interact with organization leaders in all sectors and work with OD (Organizational Development) professionals who are steeped in diagnostic rather than dialogic approaches (Bushe, 2009; Bushe & Marshak, 2009; Marshak, 2009; Marshak & Bushe, 2009; Marshak & Grant, 2011). Dialogic OD fosters the emergence of new knowledge and solutions through dialogic interaction and aligns with the dialogic and communal foundation of Indigenous learning. The dialogic OD foundation comes from the belief that each person has wisdom, and through conversation, possibilities emerge. Applicability crosses all disciplines and communities. The basic mindset blocking the emergence of people living into their potential comes from a diagnostic framework, finding the gap and fixing it vs. helping possibilities emerge. Possibilities emerge when both children and adults learn in an environment where their gifts and strengths are not only recognized but encouraged. Educators can create such an environment when they integrate Indigenous learning principles into the classroom.

The approach educators used and I experienced from a young age, diagnosing me as broken and in need of fixing, is synonymous with a diagnostic OD approach to any group of humans as a social system. For a 2e child, living this approach creates the separation and dismay coming from being treated as broken. What a horrible experience to grow up with: I know. Educators create a major roadblock to transforming education systems into social systems honoring the gifts each member of the community brings when they are steeped in a diagnostic framework. We need a shift in mindset to overcome this roadblock. Indigenous learning principles in line with dialogic OD principles, particularly spiritual ecology, communal foundation, and environmental foundation will help 2e children feel connected, nurtured, whole, and valuable. The new mindset will emerge through the co-creation of new knowledge in borderland conversations between differing worldviews. This new mindset embraces dialogue before deliberation (Figure 11.1) opening individuals and social systems to emergence.

The transmission model of communication provides much of the communication theory taught to educators. As an expert-based model, the transmission model of communication does not foster the co-creation of new knowledge. I have truth to impart and you need to listen. Then you have truth to impart, and I am to listen. Communication feels like a ping pong match with knowledge being batted back and forth. The coordinated management of meaning (CMM) school of thinking developed by Barnett Pearce (2007, 2009b) provides a healthy alternative to the transmission model of communication. CMM as a model promotes the co-creation of meaning through dialogue, an approach fully in line with Process

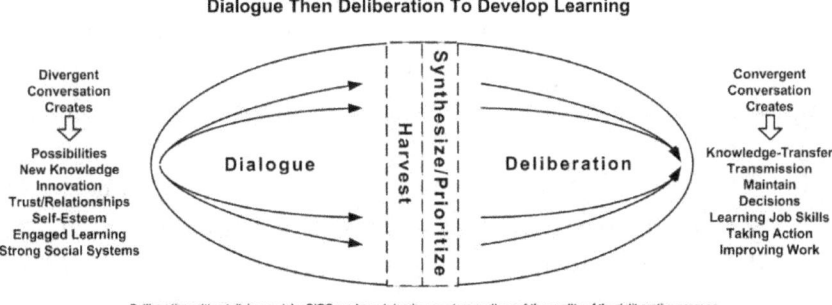

Figure 11.1 *Dialogue then deliberation model Inman, J., & Thompson, T. A. (2013).*

Organization Studies (PROS) and is the foundation for my dialogic work. A PROS mindset embraces dialogue and the co-creation of new knowledge through conversation. Rather than move directly into deliberation as we tend to do in Western cultures, it is better to open the conversation to new possibilities through dialogue and then use that output to make decisions as noted in Figure 11.1. Educators should acknowledge and embrace complexity rather than the continuous reduction of systems into parts commonly found in Western education. Introducing multiple worldviews into the curriculum, as in Indigenizing curriculum, provides an excellent way to embrace complexity, which in turn, supports 2e children who thrive in a situated complex learning environment. When embracing complexity, the expert transmission of pre-existing knowledge ignoring the reality of the world, has only a complementary role in education. When teachers become guides and participants in the learning journey, they go far beyond being the expert at the front of the room as in a dualistic framework. Indigenizing the classroom with multiple realities provides a powerful way to overcome the dualistic, right and wrong approach to knowledge found in the expert model. Had this model been in place when I was in school, a model supported by Indigenous learning principles, it would have provided me with a learning experience within which I would have thrived.

For those 2e children experiencing unhealthy education systems marked by a lack of respect for their gifts, caring support will be necessary to help them begin to believe in their potential and move beyond the belief they have no gifts. No, these children are not stupid. No, they are not lazy. No, they do not have only deficits. They have extraordinary potential and the earlier they learn to believe this, the better chance they have in developing into whole healthy human beings. When I went to FCDS, this was the help I needed to begin to heal. But even with the help I received, I have experienced lifelong discouragement. The lessons learned through fifth-grade are hard to shake and we must get to 2e children as soon as possible so that they do not have to suffer needlessly. There must be a will on the part of administrators to transform learning environments to dialogic frameworks to make this happen.

Indigenous learning foundations provide a compelling framework for change. There must be enough of us demanding these changes for the changes to be noticed and acted upon. Educators should not use a top-down expert approach. The top-down approach creates power differentials damaging learning frameworks. A co-creation model of knowledge formation works far better in a complex world. Educators can achieve this by bringing Western and Indigenous worldviews together in dialogue at the borderlands and allowing new knowledge to emerge.

Chapter 12
A Call to Action

The background has been introduced. The story has been told. The alternative picture painted. Now comes a plea for action so 2e and LD children can realize their potential and not have to wait 60 years to do so. This social justice issue must be acted on now, but a change will not be easy. Educators will struggle to turn education systems toward a more respectful and dialogic environment based on Indigenous principles, principles handed down over the millennia. One does not simply introduce a new idea and sit back and wait for it to take hold. For instance, it would be unlikely to find a more challenging example of difficult change than the volatile, uncertain, complex, and ambiguous U.S. education system. When it comes to children, emotions run high and conflicts are assured. Moving ahead will require finesse and patience, patience I do not always have. Pitfalls are numerous and offending or alienating groups a real possibility. So addressing such a daunting and pervasive social justice issue creates challenges and should not be faced alone.

I hope to address the social injustice from a lack of educational support for 2e children by designing a stepped approach to introduce new frameworks into education. But even before this call to action, a clear definition of what might roll out can paint a vision of the path. The envisioned program consists of several components. To ensure children feel like they belong and are not separated from friends, cohort grouping with a cluster grouping approach to classroom design using the school-wide cluster grouping model (SCGM) can provide the foundation. In so doing, there would not be an undue burden on a school district and only those teachers who have the talent and passion for cluster grouping work need to be trained, developed, and provided with the opportunity to take on these classrooms. In most instances, this would provide enough teachers to address all alternative learners. A team guiding and innovating the introduction of this approach would provide the breadth of knowledge and background to help secure opportunities to introduce this innovation into schools.

I foresee a substantial amount of work with a potential roll-out team exploring how to approach schools, how to format the message, how to develop a communication plan, and how to seek financial partners to help fund an initiative. It may be worthwhile to create a 501c research institute for seeking grants and donations to carry an initiative forward. Strong support would be needed to move an initiative like this forward. Partners in the team would be able to help find educators who are open to innovation leading to pilot locations. The roll-out team would set strategy and provide advice on all aspects of the initiative. Some of the steps envisioned to infuse Indigenous learning and cluster-grouped classrooms into schools follow.

The first step would start with changing the mindsets of educators to open the door to Indigenous learning principles and Indigenizing curriculum. This can be done through the introduction of multiple pathways as outlined by Baum, Viens, and Slatin (2005) positioning Indigenous learning and Indigenizing curriculum within multiple pathways. Indigenous learning foundations map directly to Gardner's entry points of narrative, foundational or existential, aesthetic, experiential or hands-on, and social (Baum, Viens, & Slatin, 2005, p. 78). I suggest using experiential workshops and dialogic processes to help teachers learn about Indigenous principles, an approach fitting philosophically with Indigenous learning. It would be necessary to have available resources and peers who have a strong grasp of the concepts to engage in conversations about the various facets of an initiative. I would develop other peers to carry the work forward in an ever-increasing spiral of energy and people with a passion for overcoming the social injustice around 2e learning in current settings. Once teachers are trained, initiating pilot projects would be the next step. Administrators would need to be heavily involved and nurtured to advocate for projects. Without administrator support, initiatives would not move forward. Publishing results and providing opportunities for peer-reviewed research and dissertations would help move these education innovations into the mainstream. With more research work being done around the initiatives, visibility of the work will increase.

Developing a research partner like Fielding Graduate University to help support the initiative would help carry forward research in Indigenous learning for 2e and other children. Having faculty support and encouragement would be important. Seeking research support would not be limited to FGU only. If these concepts could be introduced into teaching institutions responsible for the education of teachers, the long-term goal of substantial transformation of education systems would begin to be addressed. My dream would be to have this initiative live long after my ability to contribute wanes.

Part Three
A Deep Dive into Theory and Practice: What Does the Literature Say

"That is not our way, to set yourself apart and talk about who you are and what you've done. You let your life speak for you. With the Mohawk people, wisdom is how you live and how you interpret what your mother and father, what your grandmothers and grandfathers have told you about this world - and then how you interpret that into the fact of living every day."
-- -- Tom Porter, MOHAWK

Chapter 13
Foundation in Literature

To support this book, I draw from two primary bodies of theory and practice: twice-exceptional learning and Indigenous learning foundations. I also draw from Process Organization Studies (Hernes, 2008, 2010; Hernes & Maitlis, 2010), which frames my experience as a human in relationship with the world. Process Organization Studies (PROS) approaches organization studies from process metaphysics perspectives – a worldview based on processes, rather than substances, as the basic forms of the universe. A process view rests on an anti-dualist and relational ontology, recognizing nothing has existence apart from its relation to other things. PROS closely aligns with Indigenous learning foundations when it comes to viewing the world as connected and emerging.

Four Arrows and Narvaez (2015) explain a core difference in Indigenous and Western worldviews as one of language and how this creates our view of reality. Western languages are noun based and describe things and people, while Indigenous languages are verb-based and describe relationships between things and people. The Western world tends to "see" things, but this is not so in the Indigenous world where processes that cannot be seen form the foundation for communication. Four Arrows and Narvaez explain, "Indigenous ways of thinking are more concerned with the forces that interact with objects than that which can be seen with the eyes" (p. 10). PROS provides a philosophy of organization focused on how things emerge through the relationship with other things, like an Indigenous worldview. The two are complementary. When I reference PROS, I do so specifically when it supports an alternative learning paradigm based on Indigenous learning foundations.

Although the literature addresses LD and gifted learning, 2e learning, and Indigenous learning, it does not address using Indigenous learning foundations to address 2e learning. This gap in the literature provides an opportunity for this study to explore how we create new learning contexts for 2e and alternative learning children. Educators use many effective and creative educational strategies within the Western educational mindset. Adding an Indigenous learning mindset does not replace these strategies, it provides an enriched educational environment where these strategies can thrive as Indigenous learning foundations fit within the multiple pathways defined by Baum, Viens, and Slatin (2005) and reinforce and respect multiple ways of knowing the world around us in ways that have largely been lost in contemporary cultures, environments, and schooling.

Chapter 14
Twice-Exceptional Learning

2e children often fall through the gap as their gifts go unnoticed while at the same time educators not only notice but focus their energy on the child's learning disorders (Baum & Owen, 2004; Bracamonte, 2010; Brulles & Winebrenner, 2009; Winebrenner & Brulles, 2008; Yssel, Adams, Clarke, & Jones, 2014). All too often, 2e children perform at or near grade level, their gifts helping to compensate for their learning disabilities, and they end up ignored altogether (Baum, 2004; Baum & Owen, 2004; Lovecky, 2004; Montgomery, 2003; Webb et al., 2005; Winebrenner, 2003).

Several approaches have evolved to address alternative learning children. Public schools create two approaches: either in-classroom interventions or programs outside of the mainstream classroom. Both approaches could include accelerated or remedial curriculum, counseling, and so forth. Alternatively, educators set up private schools to teach gifted or learning-disabled children. Finally, parents frustrated with other options often use homeschooling. All four strategies approach education based on a dualistic Western mindset where "normal" children experience the standard curriculum, and "non-normal" children experience an altered curriculum outside of the overall design of the school educational approach and curriculum. Standardized testing serves as an example of how educators subject children to "normalized" performance measures on a bell curve.

Although educators use several approaches to provide learning environments for 2e and other students who do not fit the norm, this book focuses on in-classroom solutions negating the need to shuffle children out into alternative programs. The educational design starts with the fundamental belief that all children have gifts and those gifts need encouragement and development within the classroom in the school. It also understands that shuffling children out of classrooms makes them feel like the "other" and takes them away from their friends. Taking children out of their classrooms and away from their friends, although well-intentioned, is damaging to the self-esteem of children.

Cluster grouping educational system designs such as response to intervention (RTI) (Yssel, Adams, Clarke, and Jones, 2014) and school-wide cluster grouping model (SCGM; Brulles and Winebrenner, 2009; Winebrenner & Brulles, 2008) provide examples for in-classroom education. Cluster grouping educational system designs create a framework for teaching children at different levels of achievement in the classroom and provide a welcoming framework for the addition of Indigenous learning foundations. Yssel, Adams, Clarke, and Jones explain, "RTI – with its core principles of early intervention, high-quality instruction for all students, screening and progress monitoring and differentiated instruction – makes dual differentiation possible, and this is the environment in which students who are gifted with LD can have all their needs met and thrive" (p. 51). The school-wide cluster grouping model (SCGM; Brulles & Winebrenner; Winebrenner & Brulles) clusters several groups of students with different learning capabilities into preassigned classrooms with teachers schooled in teaching multiple levels of students within the classroom. As a more targeted model, SCGM takes fewer resources to implement in a school setting than trying to change all classrooms to accommodate 2e children. The SCGM model has the added benefit of creating cohorts of students who move through the educational system together helping create bonds and collaborative learning.

Cluster-grouped classrooms also create a multiplier effect on the number of children who can experience the transformative effects of

Indigenous learning. If we use an average of 20 students per classroom in k-12, and if five students in a cluster-grouped classroom were 2e, another 15 students would benefit from the curriculum which would have a positive impact on a broad segment of children in the school system. As well, with the SCGM model, teachers who have a talent and passion for cluster-grouped classroom education, can be specifically developed to thrive in this setting. With only a few cluster-grouped classrooms within a school, there should be little push back from teacher unions, administrators, and teachers who do not want to embrace a cluster-grouped classroom. This book suggests using the SCGM classroom design, then Indigenizing the curriculum to provide a more connected and healing approach to the world, not just a more effective Western curriculum for teaching 2e children.

Numerous resources and efforts focus on improving education for 2e children. My interest in designing the learning environment using an Indigenous worldview departs from the efforts in this field. Certainly, Indigenous educators and researchers explore Indigenizing Western education (Four Arrows, 2013; Cajete, 1994; Deloria & Wildcat, 2001; Wildcat, 2001; Wildcat & Pierotti, 2000). However, the focus has not been on alternative learning children, and in particular 2e children or why an Indigenous learning framework may uniquely adapt to this population of children. I have drawn from a variety of researchers and authors for my understanding of twice-exceptionality, learning disabilities, and gifted education and how solutions might be applied for the 2e learner. With this said, integrating Indigenous learning into a cluster-grouped classroom would probably have a positive impact on both Indigenous and non-Indigenous children. I would hope this conversation extends to both communities.

Significant Literature

Diane Montgomery's edited book *Gifted & Talented Children with Special Educational Needs: Double Exceptionality* (Montgomery, 2003) provides a substantial background for my understanding of twice-exceptional children and their learning needs. She was willing to consult with me to help me understand this evolving field and my own experiences growing up 2e. Her book provides a road map to understand gifted children who have one of several learning issues.

Educators must create a rich and engaging educational experience to keep 2e children motivated and developing into their gifts. Twice-exceptional learners often disengage in learning environments without an option to explore other worldviews, where material must be memorized, and where educators normally present data in lecture format, (Montgomery, 2003). Indigenizing education introduces a step forward in creating the cognitive challenges these children need by providing opportunities to think, create, and connect the disparate ways of knowing into new knowledge and understanding. The effort to Indigenize the curriculum increases the child's self-esteem and sense of worth to the world. Montgomery explains:

> Underlying all of these underachievements a low sense of self-esteem is to be found with a range of strategies being used to defend the sense of self or to prop it up. Characteristic also is the need in these pupils to have something interesting and challenging intellectually to engage with. But because in many classrooms the lessons are teacher led and information is imparted verbally, has to be recorded in writing and then learned, these pupils lose motivation as their involvement in making meaning for themselves diminishes. (p. 8)

Lifelong damage to self-esteem often results when children grow up being told they are lazy, have no gifts, called not bright or stupid, targeted for being different, separated away from their friends, forced into remedial programs reinforcing what they have been told and experienced, and where they struggle to keep up with their class on assignments. When 2e learners use their gifts to mask their LDs and simply achieve at average or below-average grade level, self-esteem suffers. Findings of depressed self-esteem have been substantiated in multiple studies (Chivers, 2012; Leggett, Shea, & Wilson, 2010; Nielsen & Higgins, 2005; Nielsen, 2002; Winebrenner, 2003).

Many of the strategies Montgomery uses to transform the learning settings for 2e children support the concept of Indigenizing the learning environment. One of those strategies directly supports a dialogic framework for the classroom, a strategy crucial to my proposed work in helping 2e children thrive. Montgomery (2003) says, "All these 'talking techniques' were particularly essential for dyslexic learners as part of a 'talking curriculum' in which to ground their literacy skills" (p. 47). She also stated that bright adult dyslexics "needed the support of a talking and cognitive curriculum in collaborative pairs or groups" (p. 49). The "talking curriculum" honors oral Indigenous traditions as well and authentic multicultural histories. Introducing alternative histories provides a powerful strategy for 2e children starving for a chance to do real problem-solving. Montgomery states this when she says, "People are born according to Kelly (1955) as investigative problem solvers and it was argued that student learners would also be motivated by a real problem-solving approach – and so it proved" (p. 48).

Montgomery also introduced proven interventions for helping LD children overcome their disabilities. Montgomery provides studies showing the effectiveness of Alphabetic-Phonic-Syllabic-Linguistic (APSL) programs compared with non-APSL programs. The research shows learning to spell has a strong impact on a child's ability to read but not the reverse. The progress shown in both reading and spelling in APSL programs greatly exceeds progress in non-APSL programs (Montgomery, 2003, p. 57). Strategies to help children overcome LDs combined with Indigenizing curriculum can help children develop into confident and competent learners able to contribute at high levels to help solve real-world problems.

Alphabet Children
Bright students with learning deficits
LD, GT, ADHD, ODD, GAD, EBD, and more

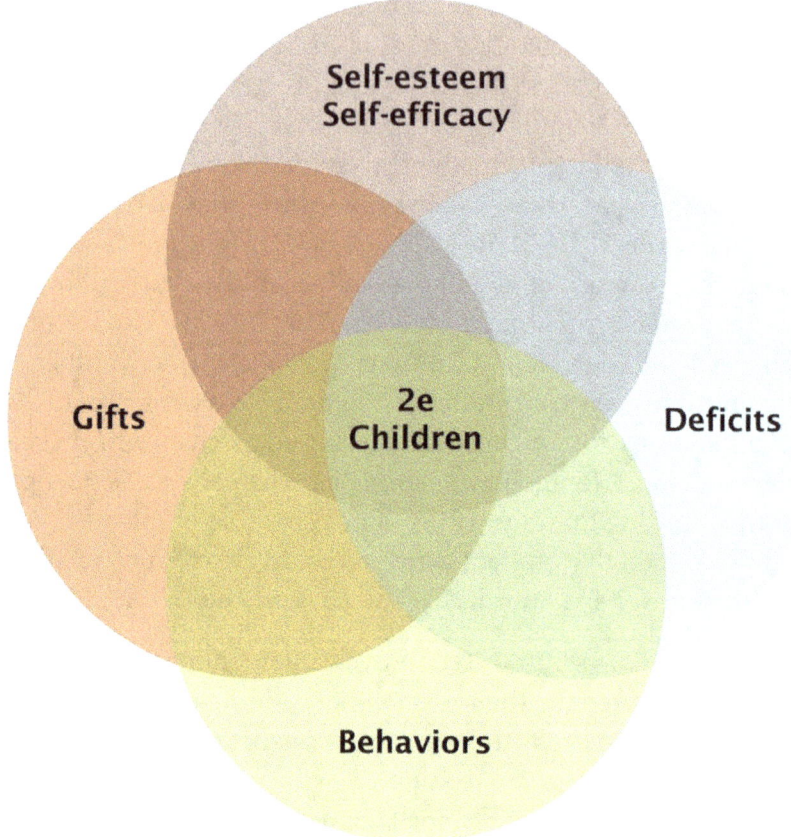

"All these disorders with contradictory and often overlapping symptoms create a serious dilemma for those seeking to provide an appropriate education." Baum, Owen

Figure 14.1 Alphabet children Baum and Owen (2004).

Susan Baum and Steven Owen (2004) in *To Be Gifted & Learning-disabled: Strategies for Helping Bright Students with LD, ADHD, and More* provide not only a comprehensive study of specific learning disabilities and giftedness but detailed strategies on how to construct educational settings to excite and engage gifted and learning-disabled (GLD) children. This text made an important contribution to my understanding of gifted education and the strategies used to help children realize their potential. As I only recognized my gifts recently, my interest in and my understanding of giftedness and gifted education emerged only after reading this book. This important addition to my education prevented inaccurate assumptions about the efficacy of current interventions for gifted children in a Western education setting.

Baum and Owen (2004) define gifted and learning-disabled children as alphabet children (Figure 14.1), as "These youngsters wind up with more letters after their names than do professionals with advanced degrees" (p. xiii). They further explain the contradictions and complexities these children bring to the classroom creating a substantial challenge for educators. Teachers find it far easier to address giftedness as an exceptionality or learning disabilities or ADHD as an exceptionality than having to deal with multiple exceptionalities in children. The contradictions generate the challenges. Although there are challenges, when educators focus on developing innate talents rather than fixing weaknesses, 2e children will thrive. I find focusing on helping children realize their gifts a similar approach to my professional work helping adults realize their potential.

My current work not only focuses on Dialogic OD (Bushe, 2009; Bushe & Marshak, 2009; Marshak, 2009; Marshak & Bushe, 2009; Marshak & Grant, 2011) as a field of practice but also on helping organizations identify natural talent in team members to help align them with work fitting their talents and strengths. Through the study of Baum and Owen (2004), I discovered this work directly aligns with educational strategies for 2e children. The more I research 2e education, the more I understand helping humans of all ages realize their potential encompasses one body of work and knowledge, developing individual gifts so people can realize their potential. In practice and philosophy, children and adults need the same recognition, encouragement, and support for their talents and strengths. Baum and Owen state, "It is increasingly clear that when the educational focus is on talent and providing learning environments that align with the student's natural ways of learning, dramatic changes occur in motivation, self-esteem, and behavior" (p. 11).

Baum and Owen (2004) provided two concepts defining children who are gifted and learning-disabled simplifying the conversation of how 2e children differ from other children. These concepts helped me explain to others in simple terms what 2e means and what it meant to me growing up as 2e. I have tried to explain this experience for years without a clear understanding of how to articulate my experience. Baum and Owen explain, "The most relevant characteristics of GLD students are specific cognitive abilities, creative tendencies, self-concept, motivation, self-efficacy, and disruptive behaviors" (p. 34). They also explain, "that GLD students are able to conceptualize and think at abstract levels. It is their poor memory for isolated facts and deficient organizational abilities that interfere with school performance" (p. 37). This last sentence describes me as a 2e learner.

The classroom strategies and development of individual learning plans for 2e children Baum and Owen (2004) outline provide a guide for ongoing work with these alternative learning children. Their conversation on measures of intelligence and recognizing intellectual strengths focused on the GLD student and WISC scores, integrative versus dispersive intelligence, and multiple intelligences. The conversation on multiple intelligences motivated me to add *Multiple Intelligences in the Classroom: A Teacher's Toolkit* (Baum, Viens, & Slatin, 2005) to my study of how to construct educational settings using Indigenous learning principles and Western strategies to excite and engage 2e children.

Susan Baum's (2004) edited volume *Twice-exceptional and special populations of gifted students* for the National Association for Gifted Children has been informative in learning about efforts in the US to understand the various populations of gifted and learning-disabled children. Her work in providing classifications of different groups of alternative learning children has helped me understand the classification of twice-exceptional children and the strategies in place to address twice-exceptionality. She specifically addresses twice-exceptional girls as a mostly ignored population.

I found Baum's (2004) conversation on enrichment programs for gifted and learning-disabled children useful. Baum and Montgomery have a similar view on children working on real-world problems rather than just being told what to believe through lectures. As mentioned above, providing alternative histories and ways of knowing the world by Indigenizing the classroom helps 2e children use their minds to solve real-world problems. The powerful strategy of offering multiple perspectives keeps children engaged and motivated while building their self-esteem. Indigenizing the classroom supports this effort (Four Arrows, 2013). Educators in the US commonly use compensation strategies to help mitigate the impact of LDs. Baum outlines the most common approaches to compensation (Baum, 2004). Educators should use these strategies in conjunction with APSL interventions to help eliminate problems rather than mask them.

Misdiagnosis and dual diagnoses of gifted children and adults (Webb et al., 2005) provided me with the background to understand the misdiagnosis of 2e children with a variety of exceptional characteristics such as ADHD, bipolar, OCD, Asperger's, depression, sleep disorders, and LDs. Surprisingly, untrained educators continue to believe gifted children cannot have LDs. Therefore, a successful introduction of Indigenizing curriculum needs a corresponding mindset shift to embrace both an Indigenous perspective and "non-normal" learning challenges in children of all backgrounds. Webb et al. (2005) states, "there appear to be far more gifted children with learning disabilities than previously thought. Most disturbingly, a significant number of educators and health care professionals have the mistaken notion a gifted child cannot have a learning disability" (p. 137). Webb et al. further state, "Gifted children with learning disabilities, if misdiagnosed, may slide into an intellectual poverty that could have been avoided. These children also have higher risks of substance abuse and psychological difficulties if their learning disability is not diagnosed and addressed" (p. 156).

Different minds: Gifted children with AD/HD, Asperger Syndrome, and other learning deficits (Lovecky, 2004) outlines traits of giftedness as well as how the brain works in different deficiencies. Several conversations in the book supported an Indigenous approach to education. The book introduces moral development directly supporting Indigenous learning, which focuses on the relationship of the individual to others, to the community, and the world. Indigenous populations view the purpose of development for the betterment of the world, not solely for personal gain as we often see in the Western world (Cajete, 1994). In Indigenous thought, honoring and respecting the gifts individuals bring and engaging in dialogue with others supports improving relationships. Emotional intelligence develops through working closely with others in a spiritual way, and cognition and respect for others improves through working through complex and real-world problems, framed through multiple ways of knowing (Four Arrows, 2013).

Lovecky (2004) addresses many specific strategies to improve learning for 2e children. Indigenizing schoolroom curriculum enhances the chance these strategies develop into a natural part of the learning environment. In advocating for twice-exceptional educational strategies almost wholly missing from many schools, Leggett, Shea, and Wilson (2010) suggest, "If such a system were to be in place and could identify and provide services for all twice-exceptional students, the positive impact of this population on modern society would be even greater than the impact made by individuals who overcome this hardship" (p. 3). Creating an educational setting based on an Indigenous framework creates an excellent context to notice and provide services for twice-exceptional children and all children.

In literature, recent studies focused on (a) classroom strategies (Brulles & Winebrenner, 2009; Chivers, 2012; Coleman, 2005; Jeweler, Barnes-Robinson, Shevitz, & Weinfeld, 2008); Nielsen, 2002; Nielsen & Higgins, 2005; Siegle & McCoach, 2005; Yssel, Adams, Clarke, & Jones, 2014; Winebrenner, 2003; Winebrenner & Brulles, 2008); (b) gifted and LD students (Lovett & Sparks, 2011); (c) social and emotional needs (Kaplan & Wiebe, 2013; King, 2005); (d) advocacy (Leggett, Shea, & Wilson, 2010); and (e) how to identify 2e children (Bracamonte, 2010; Lovett & Lewandowski, 2006; Song & Porath, 2011).

Some specific highlights of this literature supporting, if indirectly, an Indigenous framework for teaching and learning include:

- Brulles and Winebrenner (2009), Winebrenner and Brulles (2008), and Yssel, Adams, Clarke, and Jones (2014) propose providing individual learning plans for each student using cluster grouping strategies within the classroom. This approach mirrors what I would hope to create by Indigenizing the curriculum. In an Indigenous framework, children would not feel different through separation from their classmates. Although initially investing in individualized learning plans creates challenges, in the end they pay off through better student engagement and learning. A belief in developing the possibilities of every child within the classroom creates an educational setting where the school and teachers work together embracing every child's unique gifts. A dynamic and creative educational setting emerges by adding dialogic and collaborative learning strategies and an Indigenous learning foundation mindset to the classroom. Brulles and Winebrenner propose the school-wide cluster grouping model (SCGM). This creative example clusters several groups of students with different learning capabilities into preassigned classrooms with teachers trained in teaching multiple levels of students within the classroom. Yssel, Adams, Clarke, and Jones promote a multitiered approach called response to intervention (RTI). They explain, "RTI – with its core principles of early intervention, high-quality instruction for all students, screening and progress monitoring and differentiated instruction – makes dual differentiation possible, and this is the environment in which students who are gifted with LD can have all their needs met and thrive" (p. 51). Both models create an opportunity for introducing Indigenous learning foundations into the classroom.

- Chivers (2012) focuses on teacher attitudes (mindsets) and differentiating the curriculum to optimize learning for multiple ways of learning. Certainly, the focus on mindset improves the ability to Indigenize the classroom as well as alter the curriculum to meet the needs of all learners.

- Coleman (2005) suggests paying attention to four variables to ensure clear and understandable instruction. The variables include providing appropriate time for work, structure to help organize learning, sufficient support to ensure the student does not get off track, and providing complexity in the form of a relationship across ideas. Where most children can "muddle through" vague directions, 2e children cannot. An Indigenous mindset supports these educational approaches through the introduction of Indigenous enrichment strategies (the seven learning foundations, which

I explore later) and alternative worldviews into the curriculum.

- Jeweler, Barnes-Robinson, Shevitz, and Weinfeld (2008) present a learning planning card model to help a teacher easily customize the approach to each student. The Bordering on Excellence Frame tool provides areas to focus on by having the teacher circle which areas to address. This management tool helps teachers customize the curriculum for each learner in the classroom. Tools like this support Indigenous learning by helping keep track of individual learning plans.

- Nielsen (2002) and Nielsen and Higgins (2005) focus on strategies to enhance giftedness, social and emotional strategies, compensation strategies, and behavior management strategies. These strategies help customize individual learning plans for all students. In an Indigenous framework with individual learning plans supporting each child's strengths, a teacher would assume each child brings gifts and would not use labels to define the child's gift or LD.

- Siegle and McCoach (2005) address underachievement by having us understand four questions illuminating the underlying causes. Students would ask themselves, why try? Am I smart enough? Can I be successful here? and How do I put it all together? With early encouragement around these causes of underachievement, educators can create success not only for 2e children but for all children. In Indigenous settings, these strategies help ensure the teacher provides the encouragement and resources necessary to support each student's gifts.

- Winebrenner (2003) advocates teaching 2e children how they learn and to focus on the whole child, not just the gifts or the LDs. She outlines nine tips for teachers of 2e children.

    1. Teach students to appreciate individual differences.

2. Note many students who have learning difficulties approach learning globally and prefer visual and tactile-kinesthetic formats for learning success.

3. Always teach content by teaching concepts first and details second (a Gestalt approach).

4. Teach students how to set realistic short-term goals and to take credit for reaching those goals, even if they represent only a partial amount of the entire task.

5. Teach in a way tying past learning to new content.

6. Immerse all the senses in learning activities.

7. Provide specific instruction in organizational techniques.

8. Find and use any available technology to improve a student's productivity.

9. Allow students to take tests in separate, supervised environments so they can either read the test aloud to themselves or have someone else read it to them.

Teachers schooled in how to teach multiple ways of knowing the world would use all these strategies for all students. These strategies support Indigenous learning by focusing on the whole before the parts, and by focusing on the conceptual first, encouraging children to appreciate the differences and gifts each brings to the classroom. The combined strategies create a nurturing and respectful learning environment where students learn good global citizenship supporting an Indigenous mindset.

- Lovett and Sparks (2011) study 48 different researchers focused on 2e and provide a picture of how to define 2e children, detail the methodology each researcher uses, and the population of students for the study. Since the various researchers in the study define 2e slightly differently, the authors use an average cut-off of an IQ score of 120 on the

WISC-R, PIQ, VIQ, or FSIQ tests for a child to be considered 2e. Depressed IQ scores for 2e children result from the LD. So although there has been debate as to whether 2e children exist, researchers concluded these 2e children do exist and would benefit from both gifted and LD interventions. Although the study does not directly address Indigenous learning it provides a critical understanding of the target audience of my study, those educators supporting 2e children.

- Kaplan and Wiebe (2013) and King (2005) focus on the psychological well-being of 2e children. They explore building self-efficacy using positive psychology and building on strengths. The authors use the concept of signature strengths. They recommend using a strength assessment to help determine the child's strengths and then focus the curriculum on those strengths by tying the strengths to active reading. Based on their study, Kaplan and Wiebe found, "designing activities with a 2e student's Signature Strength in mind helps create activities that sustain the student's involvement. It enables us to create an educational experience that not only builds skills but bolsters students belief in their ability to complete challenging, multi-step processes" (p. 5). King finds 2e children need an educational environment focused on strengths, using enrichment activities, a nurturing environment respecting individual differences, and where educators teach compensation strategies and focus on both strengths and weaknesses. Bracamonte (2010) also addresses playing to 2e students' strengths as well as supporting emotional needs and providing counseling support. These studies support an Indigenous learning framework where educators focus on the psychological and emotional well-being of all the children in the classroom, nurturing them through encouragement, building on strengths, and not singling out those children who demonstrate differences.

- Leggett, Shea, and Wilson (2010) focus on the ethical mandate to counselors to advocate for learning environments where 2e children can excel. "When twice-exceptional students are either unacknowledged or left with unmet needs, they may be unintentionally harmed by the educational system itself. Section D.1.a of the (2010) ACSA standards states that counselors protect 'students' best interest against any infringement of their educational program" (p. 4). This study does not directly address an Indigenous framework; however, using an Indigenous framework addresses the ethical issue of ignoring or underdeveloping children regardless of their gifts. Ethical issues do exist with the current system. The current system creates the social injustice I envision addressing through the introduction of Indigenous learning foundations.

- Bracamonte (2010), Lovett and Lewandowski (2006), and Song and Porath (2011) focus on how to identify 2e students. Bracamonte finds 2e children more difficult to spot due to inconsistent performance. Twice-exceptional children do not always display giftedness, nor do they always display LDs; 2e students show strength as creative problem solvers scoring high on "WISC's spatial, pattern recognition, verbal comprehension, and abstract conceptualization measures" (Bracamonte, p. 6). Patterns of characteristics include a discrepancy between actual and expected achievement, demonstration of outstanding ability or talent, and evidence of a processing deficiency. Lovett and Lewandowski focus on the history of the understanding of 2e, present identification practices, and clinical consequences. They found identifying 2e students problematic, which causes a host of problems for schools trying to identify these children. To help schools have a consistent definition, "we should use operational definitions of giftedness and LD that are psychometrically defensible and useful for classification in school programs" (p. 524). Due to a lack of empirical research, clinicians recommend limiting assessments to defensible IQ tests and batteries of cognitive abilities. Song and Porath propose a new way to look at 2e. They question the use of LD as a viable term and instead focus on learning domains. Rather than thinking of a 2e child as disabled, as an example, they may have strong visual memory vs. auditory memory. They do not view this as a disability, only strength in a different learning domain. With this viewpoint, educators would focus on the learning domain rather than on the weakness. Song and Porath label this as giftedness in domains (GD). Educators use all these strategies to train teachers to teach in a cluster-grouped learning environment, an environment necessary for the introduction of Indigenous learning foundations. The GD strategy shows promise in supporting the introduction of an Indigenous philosophy of learning.

The 2e articles and books I explored did not address Indigenous learning foundations. Yet many of the strategies explored could have easily come from an Indigenous worldview. Some of the strategies crossing into both worldviews include collaborative process, systems models, situated problems or issues, a focus on critical thinking, using all the senses in learning, and integrated curriculum. The gap in literature and practice between twice-exceptional and Indigenous learning provided the opening for original work around my research topic, *Another Way to Understand Gifted and Dyslexic: Hypothetical Transformations via an Indigenous Worldview*.

Chapter 15
Indigenous Foundations for Education

I trust the work of two Indigenous scholars to juxtapose my autoethnographic thoughts and imaginings of what might have been. I focus on the work of Gregory Cajete and Four Arrows as I have found they have concise and clear approaches to Indigenous learning and Indigenizing education. Gregory Cajete introduced the principles upon which to base an Indigenous education in his book, *Look to the Mountain* (1994). Four Arrows defines how to Indigenize Western curriculum by infusing multiple non-Western histories and ways of knowing into the learning setting in *Teaching Truly: A Curriculum to Indigenize Mainstream Education* (2013). Both perspectives provide compelling examples of how we can transform the curriculum in schools to provide a framework for all children to realize their potential, not just 2e children such as myself.

In researching and writing on the efficacy of Gregory Cajete's work, I draw on many other Indigenous scholars, to support my understanding of his approach to traditional Indigenous education. I also reference non-Indigenous scholarship from Western researchers to provide proof of the efficacy of his approach. I do not ignore other scholars but embed their work within Gregory Cajete's work as the context for the diverse perspectives discovered in my research. I found this approach much easier for me to not only understand traditional Indigenous learning but to articulate to others its power in transforming how we teach 2e children. The seven learning foundations outlined in Cajete's work are not new as each has research and application within many educational settings. What is unique is the application of all seven learning foundations together within a non-Western context. As you review each learning foundation, do not consider whether you have used similar strategies in education, but whether you can be more effective in integrating all seven. That is the power in an Indigenous framework.

Many Indigenous scholars have written about the negative impact of providing only whitewashed perspectives of history and science. I find Four Arrows work compelling as he directly addresses how to build educational settings based on multiple perspectives honoring many ways of knowing and experiencing the world. His work is clear, well-argued, compelling, and easy to understand and follow. This does not mean, however, it will be easy to integrate as his work directly addresses the social injustices many in positions of power control. The clear articulation of these social injustices provides me with the needed language to help children experience a more just and authentic learning environment. Suggesting the addition of approaches by both Cajete and Four Arrows provides a context for transforming education for 2e children directly addressing the problems created in a Western-only approach to education.

There are many Indigenous historically proven systems of philosophy and life understanding, such as Asian, South Asian, African, Pacific, or Middle Eastern. If we dig deep into our history as a human species, we all have Indigenous roots. In the Western world, we did not start Western; rather, we started Indigenous, but somewhere along the way of developing our Western ways of knowing, we lost sight of the tens of thousands of years of knowledge about how to live in sustainable harmony with the world. We lost sight of the very essence of being human; each of us has gifts given to us by the Creator and no one has the same gifts. Indigenous learning as identified by Cajete (1994, 2005) establishes that each of us has a gift and educators must honor and develop each gift. The foundation for learning created by this Indigenous learning principle provided me with the passion to explore Indigenous learning foundations.

In my research, I have not found Indigenous learning foundations specifically applied to a subset of children such as LD or 2e children. The focus has been on Indigenizing education as a whole. Educators have a tremendous opportunity to find smaller venues where we can introduce Indigenizing principles and then let these successes move out into mainstream educational settings.

Look to The Mountain

My initial research into Indigenous learning foundations based on the work of Gregory Cajete came early in my doctoral course work. Cajete (1994) provides seven principles (Figure 15.1) respecting Indigenous learning and forming the foundation for education using Indigenous approaches.

- *Spiritual ecology*: Spiritual ecology provides the center, the place of stability, and the place from which the other six foundations emerge. Spiritual ecology represents the center of concentric circles radiating outward into wholeness.

- *Communal foundation*: When children and teachers in a community come together in dialogue to learn together, they do so in collaboration. Collaborative learning strategies engage the learner with the teacher and other learners in the learning community, so they all learn together. In a learning community, community members understand everyone teaches and everyone learns.

- *Mythic foundation*: Storytelling and myth contribute to helping a child fully integrate into her community (Cajete, 1994). The child does not grow up in this paradigm being asked to memorize disparate objective facts; instead, the family provides the context for knowledge, community, region, and the world. The child fully connects with the learning and the family designs learning activities to help integrate the child fully into the world.

126 *Indigenous Foundations for Education*

- *Affective foundation*: "This is the foundation in which we establish rapport with what we are learning and why we are learning it" (Cajete, 2005, p. 75). This foundation creates a context for the content of learning. What the child learns has a reason. We should expect children to actively participate in the community, not simply receive information we create as if they exist only as containers for our pre-existing

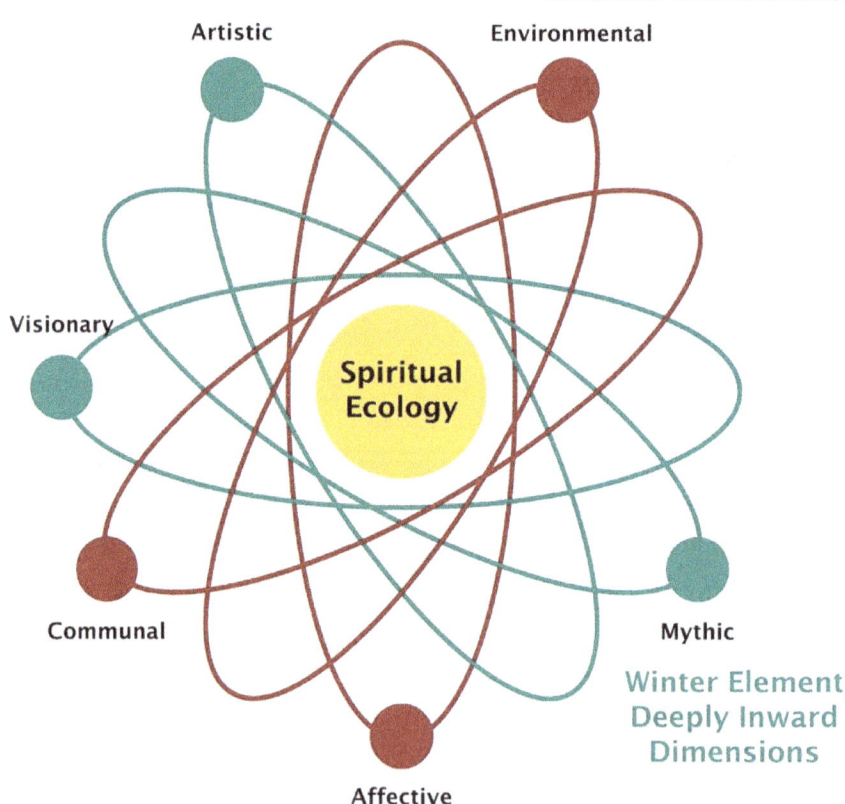

Figure 15.1 Dimensions of Indigenous education model, John Inman.

knowledge. Children need to know how they fit and how what they learn helps them integrate into the community.

- *Visionary foundation*: In Indigenous education, an important part of the journey to develop into a whole person emerges from dreaming and connecting with the non-concrete world.
- *Environmental foundation*: The world around us becomes our tutor and provides us with lessons human-generated knowledge cannot. "The Environmental foundation forms a context through which the tribe observed and integrated those understandings, bodies of knowledge, and practices resulting from direct interaction with the natural world" (Cajete, 2005, p. 74).
- *Artistic foundation*: Artistic creation closely aligns with visioning and dreaming and helps children connect with internal sources of creativity and helps them feel like whole people. "The Artistic foundation contains the practices, mediums, and forms through which we usually express the meanings and understandings we have come to see" (Cajete, 2005, p. 74).

Twice-exceptional children need to use their critical thinking skills to address complex problems. The learning environment created through the introduction of the seven learning foundations (Cajete, 2005) creates a setting where these children can thrive. Twice-exceptional children see the world as connected and connection forms the foundation for learning. They think out of the box and do not fit the norm. Indigenous learning foundations support and encourage 2e children to explore and fully develop their unique gifts. Twice-exceptional children also have a deep desire for social justice and fostering spiritual connections support this focus. Learning in a setting as outlined by Cajete requires a framework where each child can grow and develop without ever feeling broken and in need of fixing. In creating such an environment, all children would end up benefiting, not just the 2e children. Educators can start to create such an environment by recognizing 2e children have been a neglected population of children even with little agreement on how to initially move forward. Real change can happen at this borderland when educators introduce an Indigenous learning environment.

Teaching Truly

Many 2e children see in patterns. They see through shallow explanations and experience frustration by having information withheld from them. Having only one point of view presented inherently withholds information. They want the challenge of exploring contradictions, complexity, and multiple ways of knowing the world. Examples in the Western world of notable people thought to have been 2e and on their own overcame the roadblocks and have led changes in the world include Leonardo da Vinci, Thomas Alva Edison, Albert Einstein, Auguste Rodin, Charles Marion Russell, Hans Christian Andersen, and Agatha Miller Christie. Autobiographical descriptions of gifted and dyslexic individuals include Charles Schwab, John Irving, Jay Leno, and William Hewlett (Leggett, Shea, & Wilson, 2010; Song & Porath, 2011). Transforming the way we educate 2e children reduces or eliminates roadblocks.

I envision removing roadblocks so all 2e children can contribute to their families, communities, and the world at a high level. Four Arrows (2013), in *Teaching Truly: A Curriculum to Indigenize Mainstream Education,* introduces a prototype to provide contradictions, complexity, and multiple ways of knowing the world into each Western topic now provided in the Western educational setting. He builds a convincing argument that the dualistic and linear Western model of education promotes corporate and hegemonic interests at the expense of creating a learning culture based on discovery and dialogue. Children find it difficult to discover new knowledge through dialogic experiences when told only one right answer exists and educators shovel the one right answer into children as if empty buckets (Freire, 2009). Often the one right answer oppresses or keeps other worldviews out of sight or out of mind where dialogic processes lead to emancipation for all participants allowing them to fully explore all aspects of an issue or question. Four Arrows (2014) explains how this dualistic pattern propagates and explains an alternative when he says,

> Educational assumptions about capitalism, privatization, globalization, free markets, continual growth, consumerism, and even prosperity are ideas too few in educational circles question because there is not a conceptual, proven alternative worldview to help us awaken to the false assumptions of the dominant one. Such a worldview exists in the Indigenous ways of understanding life, ways that are common denominators in most if not all Indigenous cultures. (p.31)

The approach suggested by Four Arrows would provide 2e children with a rich and engaging educational environment where they can use their gifts to the fullest and where they can begin to establish new knowledge capable of helping us heal the world. Jeweler, Barnes-Robinson, Shevitz, and Weinfeld (2008) explain:

> A major goal of education is to provide all students with the opportunity to reach their potential. Although few are able to argue with this goal, twice-exceptional students, including some of our most gifted students, are often on the brink of excellence due to the unique blend of assets and deficits they exhibit. Teachers are challenged each day to find ways to empower those bright students who may be unable to write a complete sentence, even though they are able to participate actively in a class discussion. These are the students who may not be able to read a science textbook but may show their knowledge of physics by constructing an elaborate model of a roller coaster that demonstrates the concepts of friction and centrifugal force. (p. 41)

One can only imagine the 2e people who have changed the world and come from other backgrounds without being recognized by Western scholars. Educators may miss or forget 2e children, but 2e children coming from minority backgrounds have all but disappeared from the radar. From a social justice perspective, when educators use an Indigenous approach to education as an important addition to the conversation, we can begin to provide children of all backgrounds and ways of knowing the world with an opportunity to learn and realize their potential. Four Arrows (2013) asks then answers, "How can such a theory of learning be adopted and adapted by mainstream education? One way is to not look at the curriculum as something to cover but rather as a catalyst for discovery" (p. 65). Educators must make a shift in worldview to transform education into a catalyst for discovery and an Indigenous philosophy of education provides a framework for this shift.

Cajete (1994, 2005) suggests educators use art as an important element to create this transition. Not as a tack-on class often removed at every budget impasse, but an integral part of the curriculum helping children learn and grow. Four Arrows, in Four Arrows, Cajete, and Lee (2010) explains, "Art, and I include music when I say art, to Indigenous cultures is not a form of entertainment, amusement or escape as it often is in dominant cultures. Art represents creations that define place and lead to transformations" (p. 88). Twice-exceptional learners need educators to infuse foundations such as art back into the curriculum as Four Arrows suggests. Twice-exceptional learners also demonstrate the ability to creatively synthesize disparate inputs. When educators provide strategies to expand the ability for these children to contribute through redesign of the curriculum, the new environment helps the children connect the disparate inputs from multiple ways of knowing Four Arrows recommends and begin to develop new knowledge. This mode of discovery energizes 2e learners. Four Arrows explains, "Indigenous learning traditionally is about discovery, symbols, metaphors, even dreams. It was fully holistic, which is largely a right brain way of seeing the world" (Four Arrows, Cajete, & Lee, 2010, p. 121). Educators create the opposite of the linear rational Western model of education when they infuse Indigenous learning into the classroom. I recommend educators explore these strategies for 2e learning environments to provide the enrichment needed for these children to realize their potential.

Summary of Literature

I found extensive research and application of innovative approaches to teaching gifted children, learning-disabled children, and gifted and learning-disabled children. Some approaches focus on separate programs and others on cluster-grouped classrooms. In every case, the solutions are situated within the Western dualistic and mechanistic worldview. So although any single approach might positively alter the course of a child's learning experience, none of them address the power of adding a non-Western worldview to the education system. They all propose strategies embedded in a Western worldview. Indigenous learning strategies and literature on Indigenizing curriculum did not address how to use these strategies to address specific groups or classrooms. The framework I have proposed does exactly that.

While compelling, I found the breadth of Indigenous strategies to be overwhelming and difficult to approach. The strategies did not address specific groups such as those addressed in the gifted, learning-disabled, and gifted and learning-disabled literature. Each body of research addresses specific frameworks, but none integrates the two bodies of research and work together. The literature gap manifests in each body of work; however, the major gap comes from a lack of integration of the two bodies of work. This integration makes the Indigenous scholarship broadly accessible and enhances the strategies of alternative learning instruction to have more impact and better outcomes.

Part Four
Indigenous Learning and the Theories Supporting It

"Respect should be given those indigenous nations who still carry on their ceremonies; still following the ancient laws of nature with songs and ceremonies."
-- -- *Oren R. Lyons, Spokesman, Traditional Circle of Elders*

Chapter 16
Indigenous World View of Education

Indigenous educational principles, regardless of the tribal source, consistently embrace a holistic worldview and respectfully embrace the differences individuals bring to the learning journey (Cajete, 1994). Educators can develop healthy and engaged children through the integration of Indigenous learning into educational settings. We cannot expect educators to accept the introduction of these principles into classrooms without justification to support the efficacy of the solutions. I designed the work in this book to help provide this justification. Even with the support of my research, change will be difficult as problems in the education system are deep and challenging. "Even a cursory examination of the numerous problems facing modern technological societies and the failure of modern education systems to find solutions to these problems, which are essentially moral and ethical in character, suggests something is fundamentally amiss in the dominant educations systems of the United States" (Wildcat, 2001, p. 7). Senge (2000), when talking about the barriers to change the industrial age system of education, explains:

> The assumption of smart and dumb kids is so deeply ingrained in our society that it is hard to imagine an alternative. But the alternative is right before us: All human beings are born with unique gifts. The healthy functioning of any community depends on its capacity to develop each gift. When we hold a newborn we do not see a smart or a dumb kid. We see the miracle of life creating itself. The loss of that

awareness is the greatest toll exacted by our prevailing system of education, in and out of school. (p. 42)

A Holistic View of the Learner and Their Environment

We live in a Western positivist culture defined by a dualistic approach to the world. According to Boyte (2009), positivism is threatening our destruction. He suggests, "Even though it has long been discredited intellectually, positivism continues to structure our research, our disciplines, our teaching, and our institutions of higher education" (p. 11). Humans in the Western culture separate and disconnect from the world, observing and using the physical world without connecting to it (Capra, 1996; Macy, 1991; Senge, 1990; Skyttner, 2008; Wheatley, 1999). As we explore aspects of Indigenous traditions regarding education, we find the foundation of the Indigenous approach holistic and spiritually connected. Cajete (2006) explains, "Deep understanding of relationships and the significance of participation in all aspects of life are key to traditional American Indian education. 'Mitakuye Oyasin' (we are all related), a Lakota phrase, means that our lives are truly and profoundly connected to other people and the physical world" (p. 56). This book asserts that starting 2e children on an educational journey feeling fully connected to the world reduces the anxiety and sense of separation felt by these children. If children start out feeling fully connected to others and the world, they may never develop a deep sense of feeling different from other children. We manufacture things in the Western positivist culture. Our growth and progress derive from our ability to manufacture stuff. Unfortunately, Western culture set up the education system to manufacture educated children. Herein lies the source of the problem.

Children like other biological systems represent living systems (Capra, 1996, 2002; Senge, 2000; Macy, 1991; Wheatley, 1999) and do not thrive in a mechanistic approach to developing into whole and healthy humans. In a mechanistic system, educators try to drive variability out of the system to create children who all have the same knowledge. Our children cannot achieve this level of consistency and I suggest we should not have this as a goal. When we see children as unique living systems, we open the opportunity to help them develop the confidence to think completely and make wise choices, speak with responsibility, and act decisively for the good of the world. I and others who grow up 2e find themselves in the broken pile to be remanufactured to meet specifications. Indigenous education principles provide another way to create learning, one embracing a living systems approach. Senge (2000) summarizes his thoughts about restructuring education around a living systems model: "Learning is nature's expression of the search for development. It can be diverted or blocked, but it can't be prevented from occurring. The core educational task in our time is to evolve the institutions and practices that assist, not replace, that natural learning process" (p. 57).

Cajete (2006) paints a picture of education based on a natural learning process "designed to encompass important ancestral traditions; emphasize respect for individual uniqueness in diverse spiritual expressions; facilitate understanding of history and culture; develop a strong sense of place and service to community; and forge a commitment to educational and social transformation" (p. 56). Exploring what education might look like based on these principles, keeps in mind this socially situated holistic approach to 2e children.

The way educators communicate to children has an impact on developing their worldview and helping them feel connected to all people, human and non-human. Macdonald (2009) suggests educators pay attention to the barriers created by language constructed toward 2e children. Those living in Western culture have a long history of constructing language from a mechanistic point of view. The Indigenous learning paradigm does not include mechanistic language. It will be difficult for educators to create a shift in language to honor a holistic approach to learning. This book recommends a change of language and a focus on dialogue to help transform the classroom into one helping 2e children realize their potential. Gordon (2007), in quoting Gordon (2006), provides a picture of difficulty to move in this direction:

> Infrequently in our mainstream Western journals and texts do we see work in the area of spiritual communication, or communication with nature. The fact that our underlying models and discourse for thinking about and describing communication originally came from the engineering sciences and pertained to machine-to-machine and person-to-machine communication has historically made it difficult to move outside our mechanistic discourse and construe larger organic possibilities. (p. 98)

The Indigenous epistemologies forming the foundation of the recommended educational paradigms use more holistic and inclusive language. Although "there is no word for epistemology in any American Indian language" (Cajete, 2005), understandings do exist informing how to talk about Indigenous educational concepts (Zimmerman, 2004). The first understanding embraces the holistic approach to education. Cajete explains, "American Indian education historically occurred in a holistic social context that developed a sense of the importance of each individual as a contributing member of the social group" (p. 69).

The holistic framework of Indigenous education solidly aligns with modern systems theory. Long before Bogdanov (1980) created his systems theory of tektology in the 1920s and long before Von Bertalanffy (1969) first outlined general systems theory in the 1940s, Indigenous people had lived deep spiritual systems practices for thousands of years. Where we now discover systems thinking, systems thinking was a foundation of Indigenous living and provided the foundation for Indigenous education. "The environment was not something separate from their lives, but was the context, the set of relationships, that connected everything" (Cajete, 1994). Luhmann (1995) translates systems thinking into a social systems framework based on conversations and relationships with those in the community. Understanding how social systems work helps to create critical learning cultures for 2e children, cultures that recognize these children as whole contributing persons in the complex world. "To overcome our Cartesian anxiety, we need to think systemically, shifting our conceptual focus from objects to relationships" (Capra, 1996, p. 295). Understanding complexity helps these children see the paradox of a right and wrong way of being and realize this paradox as part of living in a complex world.

Unlike in Western positivist paradigms, Indigenous traditions support multiple truths, not just one scientific truth. If educators expect to connect with children who see the world differently, Western education systems must understand that reliance on a single objectivist model does not accurately reflect reality. "it is one thing to impose a single objectivist model in some restricted situations and to function in terms of that model – perhaps successfully; it is another to conclude that the model is an accurate reflection of reality" (Lakoff & Johnson, 1980, p. 221). Palmer (1998) explains, "No scientist knows the world merely by holding it at arm's length: if we ever managed to build the objectivist wall between the knower and the known, we could know nothing except the wall itself" (p. 54). 2e children have a different way of knowing the world and providing them with the space to have different ways of knowing provides an important component of their education. "By relaxing the conscious mind's hold on reality, a person becomes aware of circles, learns to tolerate paradoxes, and realizes that no one way need exclude others in order to be true" (Nelson, 1993, p. 16).

Twice-exceptional children develop into powerful advocates for the healing of the world when educators provide a focus on embracing a holistic worldview. "To build a sustainable society for our children and future generations, we need to fundamentally redesign many of our technologies and social institutions so as to bridge the wide gap between human design and the ecologically sustainable systems of nature" (Capra, 2002, p. 99). Indigenous educational principles provide this framework. When educators structure an engaging educational paradigm for 2e children using a holistic approach based on conversations and relationships with all human and non-human persons, it helps these children feel part of this extraordinary world and know their unique way of knowing is valid and important. In Indigenous mythology, all of creation has a right to exist on its terms; this is where personhood for non-humans comes into play. As Meadows (2008) states, "Remember, always, that everything you know, and everything everyone knows, is only a model" (p. 172), and embracing multiple models help 2e children feel whole on their journey to develop as contributing human beings.

Indigenous Foundation for Learning

Indigenous learning derives from a deep connection with the universe. No dualistic view of human beings as separate from all else blocks a sense of relationship and family in Indigenous learning (Zimmerman, 2004). This sense of relationship and family extends to both humans and non-humans (Cajete, 1994). Those who want to emulate the sense of ecology found in Indigenous traditions but do so from a Western positivist perspective, do not understand the Indigenous connection with place. It is not ownership of or stewardship over the land, world, and universe forming the Indigenous sense of ecology, but a connection with and love of family. A learning relationship with the whole integrates several inner and outer realities of learners and teachers. Cajete (2005) introduces us to these realities:

> *Hah oh* is a Tewa phrase sometimes used to connote the process of learning. Its literal translation is to breathe in. *Hah oh* is an Indian metaphor that describes the perception of traditional tribal education – a process of breathing in – that each tribe creatively and ingeniously applied. As a whole, traditional tribal education revolved around experiential

learning (learning by doing or seeing), storytelling (learning by listening and imagination), ritual or ceremony (learning through initiation), dreaming (learning through unconscious imagery), the tutor (learning through apprenticeship), and artistic creation (learning through creative synthesis). (p. 72)

Cajete (1994, 2005) provides the above framework for understanding the full ecology of Indigenous education based on the seven-direction model forming the foundation for most traditions. The seven foundations of Indigenous education providing one of the frameworks for this book honors the seven-direction model. Cajete (1994) explains, "The majority of American Indian tribes recognize seven sacred or elemental directions. These directions include East, West, North, South, Zenith, Nadir, and the Center. Through deep understanding and expression of the metaphoric meaning of these orientations, American Indians have intimately defined their place in the universe" (p. 37). The seven learning foundations based on these elements include environmental, mythic, visionary, artistic, affective, and communal. Spiritual ecology provides the seventh learning foundation central to the others. Cajete (2005) defines the outcome of Indigenizing Western education:

> A primary orientation of indigenous education was that each person was in reality his or her own teacher and that learning was connected to each individual's life process. One looked for meaning in everything, especially in the workings of the natural world. All things of Nature were teachers of humankind; what was required was a cultivated and practiced openness to the lessons that the world had to teach. Ritual, mythology, and the art of storytelling combined with the cultivation of relationship to one's inner self; individuals used the family, the community, and the natural environment to help realize their potential for learning and a complete life. Individuals were enabled to reach completeness by being encouraged to learn how to trust their natural instincts, to

listen, to look, to create, to reflect and see things deeply, to understand and apply their intuitive intelligence, and to recognize and honor the spirit within themselves and the natural world. This is the educational legacy of indigenous peoples. It is imperative that we revitalize its message and its way of educating for life's sake at this time of ecological crisis. (p. 77)

Spiritual Ecology

Holistic Indigenous education does not have the positivist and dualistic baggage Western education contains. But holistic does not quite capture the spiritual nature of learning in Indigenous learning as spirit frames the "why" in all learning. We learn as a spiritual act for the good of the community and creation, not for personal gain. We learn to improve ourselves in the Western paradigm; spirituality has little or no place in the quest for knowledge. Cajete (1994) explains, "For Indian people, traditional learning begins and ends with the spirit. It is an old maxim that puts in context what Indigenous people view as education. The perspective incorporates the metaphors of Pathway, orientation, hunting, and seeking life and completeness into a system and a symbolic language for education" (p. 69).

Some people in Western culture might react poorly to a conversation about including spiritual ecology at the center of an educational framework. The foundation of these feelings comes from a Western positivist culture separating people from the world and universe and certainly separating people from those aspects of the universe, which cannot be objectively defined and observed. The reason we have children who feel disconnected, different, and lack a sense of place and purpose in the world comes from this dualistic cultural foundation. Religion is not the same as a conversation about spirituality. There was not a concept for religion in Indigenous beliefs. Allen (1998) explains, "For tribal peoples, spirituality and mysticism are communitarian realities. The community and every individual within it must ever be mindful of the human obligation to spirit, balance, and the relationship (on kinship) that exists among all beings, so that all might prosper" (p. 47).

Spiritual ecology provides the center, the place of stability, and the place from which the other six foundations emerge. Spiritual ecology forms the center of concentric circles radiating out into wholeness. "What seems to have been intact in all these settings were the concentric circles of interconnection – the campfire, the extended family, the larger society, humanity, nature, and the mystery of Spirit" (Baldwin, 1998, p. 27). Without spiritual ecology, one would simply implement disparate strategies without a tight interconnection and purpose to the greater good of humanity, the earth, and the universe. If we want to develop children who can unleash and realize their power and creativity, having a deep sense of spiritual connection must be central to the effort. In Indigenous terms, this is living a good life.

Cajete, in Four Arrows, Cajete, and Lee (2010), tells us, "The Indigenous ideal of living a good life in Indian traditions is sometimes referred to as striving to 'always think the highest thoughts.' This metaphor refers to the framework of a sophisticated epistemology of community based ecological education" (p. 140). Children with a spiritual connection can tune in to the world and unleash their creative selves to help solve the pressing problems humanity faces. These children do not rigidly stick to a dualistic paradigm, they instead bring agility and a keen ability to think clearly and fluently to help their near and far family in a dynamic world. Staying focused on spiritual ecology helps 2e children live a good life and fulfill their journey to develop into whole contributing persons.

To inform my learning and the learning of others, I created the model in Figure 16.1 of concentric rings founded on spiritual ecology. This model provides three paths from spiritual ecology radiating out to wisdom. Each helps learners lead a good life, realize

144 *Indigenous World View of Education*

their potential, and keeps spirit at the center of learning. Each of the three paths provides a journey founded on concentric rings like the journey from a spiritual connection to self, family, community, and the world but in this case, focused on a learning journey. Keeping

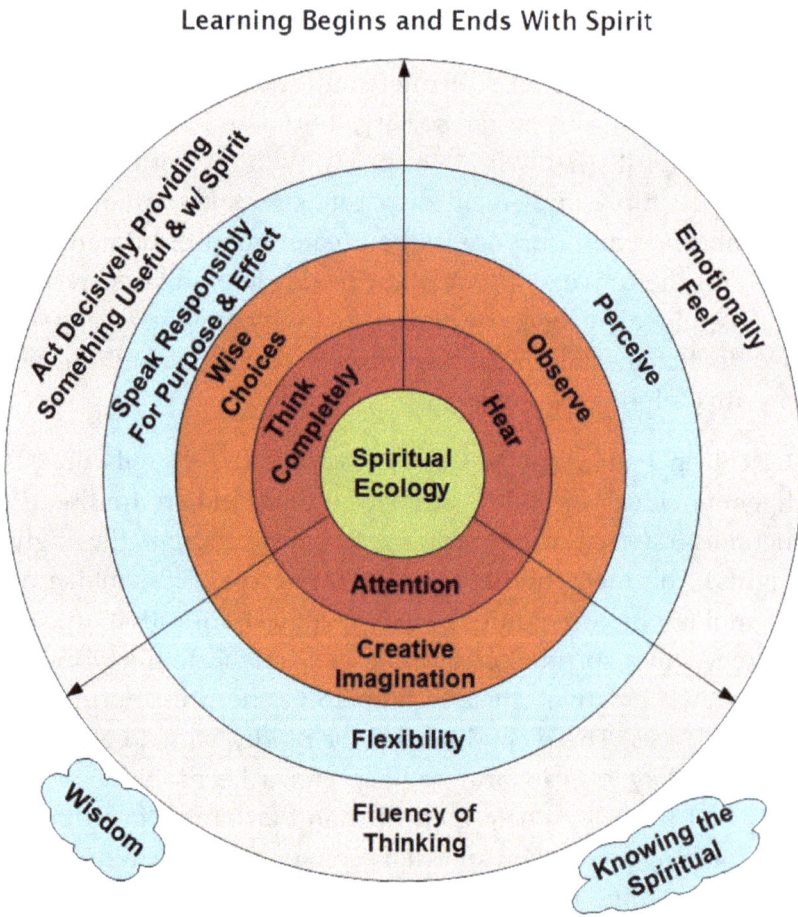

Figure 16.1 Education is process of following tracks/multiple pathways, John Inman.

these paths central to a 2e child's learning helps the child connect their experience with the spiritual and the world and understand their place in the universe.

Keeping spirit at the center of learning does not conflict with the religious traditions a child may bring to the classroom as spiritual ecology is not a religion and does not inhibit the practice of one's faith (Cajete, 1994). However, it does provide a context for personal faith to manifest for the good of humanity, the world, and the universe. Having a strong and stable center from which to learn and grow has a profound impact on a 2e child's ability to learn, grow, and experience wholeness in the journey to develop into a complete human in the world. The circle is an ancient model of how humans come together. Black Elk speaks through Neihardt (1988) telling the importance of the circle when he says,

> Everything the Power of the World does is done in a circle. The sky is round, and I have heard that the earth is round like a ball, and so are all the stars. The wind, in its greatest power, whirls. Birds make their nests in circles, for theirs is the same religion as ours. The sun comes forth and goes down again in a circle. The moon does the same, and both are round. Even the seasons form a great circle in their changing, and always come back again to where they were. The life of a man is a circle from childhood to childhood, and so it is in everything where power moves. (p. 194)

Experiential learning and the communal foundation

Humans learn best when in an experiential setting (Kolb, 1984). In the Western dualistic paradigm, one would sit back and observe or be given objective knowledge to be added to the mental database (Capra, 1996; Macy, 1991; Palmer, 1998; Senge, 1990; Skyttner, 2008; Wheatley, 1999). Many of us have experienced the lecture format of education. The expert, the person in front of the uneducated students, imparts knowledge and wisdom to those who do not know. Objective knowledge must be learned, and someone must teach it. The objectivist approach has a distinct downside and does not honor Indigenous ways of knowing. "Dominant models of knowledge making [found in the Western positivist worldview] undercut the moral and civic authority of forms of knowledge that are not academic – wisdom passed down by cultural elders, spiritual insight, local and craft knowledge, the common sense of a community" (Boyte, 2009, p. 2). In contrast, in an experiential setting, the teacher certainly has knowledge and wisdom to offer but becomes a part of the learning community rather than separate from it.

Creating shared meaning through dialogue forms the foundation of both experiential and Indigenous learning. "Indian community is the primary context for traditional education. Community is the context in which the affective dimension of education unfolds" (Cajete, 1994). Dialogue provides the foundation for creating a sense of community. Bohm (2008), when talking about the role of dialogue in creating shared meaning in a community says, "It's something new, which may not have been in the starting point at all. It's something creative. And this shared meaning is the 'glue' or 'cement' that holds people and societies together" (p. 7). Children also learn how to relate to the people and the world around them within the context of dialogue in a community. Lyle (2000), in relating to what Mead in his description of symbolic interaction says, "He suggested that children bring into the world powerful social tendencies that impel them to participate in a community: it is through social activity and exchanges that children are able to take on roles, put themselves in the place of another person and make inferences concerning the others' experiences" (p. 51).

When children and teachers in a community come together in dialogue to learn together, they do so in collaboration. Educators design collaborative learning strategies into the curriculum so everyone learns together by engaging the learner with the teacher and other learners in the learning community. Everyone teaches and everyone learns in a learning community reducing the power differential found in lecture-formatted classrooms. In his groundbreaking work on education, Freire (Freire & Faundez, 1989; Freire, 2009) provided a framework for reducing the power differentials normally found in educational settings. In this setting, the teacher creates containers for collaboration and dialogue and fosters learning conversations. Later work on conversation as experiential learning by Baker, Jensen, and Kolb (2002) provides a strong case for conversation as an experiential approach to learning. Conversational learning supports Indigenous communal learning and provides a theoretical foundation for the experiential communal learning models found in Indigenous education. Rogers (1995) supports learning as experience when he explains:

> If we accept Dewey's definition of education as the reconstruction of experience, what better way can a person learn than by becoming involved with his whole self, his very person, his root drives, emotions, attitudes and values? No series of facts or arguments, no matter how logically or brilliantly arranged, can even faintly compare with that sort of thing. (p. 306)

It takes courage for a teacher to give up the power of being the expert. Many teachers would find it easier to simply remain at the head of the class and impart wisdom and knowledge to the containers in the room, the students. Freire (2009) calls this the banking approach to education and this banking approach to education provides another example of how Western education sees the child as separate from the world. "Implicit in the banking concept is the assumption of a dichotomy between human beings and the world: a person is merely *in* the world, not *with* the world or with others; the individual is a spectator, not re-creator" (p. 75). A great return awaits teachers who step out of this framework, embrace dialogue as a foundation for learning, and willingly give up the expert power position as the sole educational approach to teaching. When they do so, they will receive the gift of healthy children who embrace complexity, confidently engage, and develop into contributing members of the world. To help 2e children in the Western positivist culture, educators must embrace collaborative classroom strategies. When educators create a learning community honoring every child's contribution, wisdom, and ways of knowing, the act of singling out children who learn differently disappears. Educators instead recognize and embrace each child's unique gifts. Freire, in Freire and Macedo (1995), explains the personal importance of dialogue from his perspective as a teacher:

> I engage in dialogue not necessarily because I like the other person. I engage in dialogue because I recognize the social and not merely the individualistic character of the process of knowing. In this sense, dialogue presents itself as an indispensable component of the process of both learning and knowing. (p. 379)

When Hillary Clinton said, "It takes a village to raise a child" many in the Western positivist culture were upset (Clinton, 1996). The statement she chose comes from an ancient African proverb, which is a concept as basic to humans as being human. In an Indigenous educational setting, every person in the tribe teaches the child. The whole community takes responsibility to raise children in a nurturing and caring manner. Many of the Western practices causing 2e children to feel isolated, different, and inferior came to the US with the colonizers. The practices were not part of American Indian education (Allen, 1992, 1998; Cajete, 1994; Deloria & Wildcat, 2001; Four Arrows, 2013). The tribe embraced the difference in each child as each of them had special talents. Adults did not tell children they were not normal, not the same, or not a value to the tribe. Tribal members allowed children to learn at their own pace and embraced their special talents. Children had the potential of growing into healthy and contributing members of the tribe. Western educators should insure each 2e child feels the same sense of belonging.

In a communal experiential setting, educators do not have to move everyone at the same pace. Trying to ensure every child gets the same objective knowledge at the same time ends up doing damage to 2e children. In a collaborative setting, children help each other and learn from each other at their own pace reducing the stigma of not being the same. An educator can deliberately create this type of experiential setting, a learning community where children learn together. The help of my friends provided one of the ingredients helping me to survive through the fifth-grade while not being able to read. Children can be wonderful and nurturing if educators create this culture in the classroom. Cajete (2005) says, "For American Indian tribal education, the community was and continues to be the schoolhouse!" (p. 76).

Storytelling and the mythic foundation

We humans learn through stories. "Students of literature . . . are so conscious of narrative that some have argued it is storytelling which makes us human" (Landau, 1984, p. 262). And Cajete (1994) says, "Humans are storytelling animals. Story is a primary structure through which humans think, relate, and communicate. We make stories, tell stories, and live stories because it is such an integral part of being human" (p. 116). And Egan (1991) states, "We are a storying animal; we make sense of things commonly in story forms; ours is a largely story-shaped world" (pp. 96-97). Educators in the Western world have focused education on the transmission method of communication (Pearce, 2007); students should listen and receive the objective truth from the teacher (Lyle, 2000). Storytelling provides the foundation for Indigenous learning and our roots as humans. We learn best from stories and ongoing research supports the efficacy of using storytelling in the classroom (Lyle): "only recently have some Western scholars of myth begun to cultivate an appreciation for these keepers, and reverence for the *power* of myths in shaping human learning and experience" (Cajete, p. 115).

Storytelling and myth contribute to helping children become fully integrated into the community (Cajete, 1994). The child does not grow up in this paradigm asked to memorize disparate objective facts; instead, knowledge of the family, community, region, and the world provides the context for learning. Educators design learning to help children connect and integrate into the world. As Pearce (2007) states, "Both the story told, and the manner of its telling are part of the creation of the social worlds in which we all live" (p. 217). The power of myth as story connects children to the world around them. No longer do children feel different and disconnected to the world; instead, they feel fully connected and a part of the world. Cajete explains the power of myth in learning as follows:

> Living through myth means using the primal images that myth presents in a creative process of learning and teaching that connects our past, present, and future. Living through myth also means learning to live a life of relationships to ourselves, other people, and the world based on appreciation, understanding, and guidance from our inner spirit and our wealth of ancestral and cultural traditions. (p. 116)

Schools need teachers willing to step out of the transmission mode of teaching and creatively draw children into a fully connected world. Developing a deep connection with the world removes the separation experienced in the Western education system by 2e children feeling different and in need of fixing. Mythology does this for children. Mythology helps children use all their senses to tune in to the world around them. Stories help them better observe the world and gain a sense of how they are a part of the world. At a deep level, they feel connected and a part of a fully connected world.

To use heroic myth in the classroom, educators must step out of the American view of myth as a lie (Allen, 2002, p. 102) and understand the pivotal role myth plays in helping us become fully connected humans in the world. Thomas Mann (1960), as quoted by

Allen states, "The myth is the legitimization of life; only through and in it does life find self-awareness, sanction, consecration" (p. 104). Children love and connect to mythic stories telling of the hero's journey. Mythic stories such as these provide a powerful way to connect to children and connect children to their world. Often comics play this role for children. But teachers rarely bring comics and the comic mythic storyline into the classroom. These heroic stories engage children in ways assimilation of objective knowledge does not and they also similarly connect concept and participation. In Indigenous learning, heroic figures in myth regularly integrate into the child's learning. Allen further explains, "An American Indian myth is a story that relies preeminently on symbol for its articulation. It generally relates a series of events and uses supernatural, heroic figures as the agents of both the events and the symbols. As a story, it demands the immediate, direct participation of the listener" (p. 104).

Lyle (2000), in exploring how to integrate narrative into the classroom, found a strong foundation in Western research supporting the use of myth. The research of Egan (1992) provides insights to educators who want to integrate Indigenous storytelling approaches into the classroom. Lyle notes in Egan (1992) children's imaginations are stimulated by emotions (p. 56). Egan states, "The tool we have for dealing with knowledge and emotions together is the story" (p. 71). To integrate myth and storytelling into education, teachers should not eliminate the Western positivist perspective, only keep it in balance with alternate ways of knowing. As Nelson (1993) explains, "The task is not to abandon science or analytic thought, but to have it take its proper place in relationship to other realities" (p. 5). Nelson further explains, "It is not a matter of teaching people the one other reality; it is rather a matter of teaching people to experience multiple realities" (p. 11). The 2e child without this balance in ways of knowing feels disconnected and broken in a Western positivist world. Educators must bring balance to these children by fully integrating myth and storytelling into their learning experience.

Ritual or ceremony and the affective

Rituals fill the lives of humans. Common human rituals include the way we get up in the morning and get ready for the day, the educational structures for children, how we eat meals together if we do, sporting events, and religious ceremonies. Humans easily embrace rituals even though many rituals are automatic, and we do not seem to notice them. Rituals help children feel like they belong to something greater than themselves. Rituals connect children with the community and create an emotional bond to the community. As Cajete (2005) states when describing the affective, "this is the foundation in which we establish rapport with what we are learning and why we are learning it" (p. 75). Rituals provide the foundation and context for what children learn. When teachers use ritual to reinforce the classroom, they help create learning with a purpose. Children actively contribute to the community and need to understand how they fit and how what they learn helps them become an integral part of the community.

Rituals as episodes of communication let children participate in this special type of story. But unlike an unstructured story, humans fully plan some rituals. As Pearce (2007) states when describing a church service, "There are no hard choices or moments of uncertainty" (p. 151). Yet humans organize rituals such as games and sporting events and these rituals, although structured, do have flexibility on how they roll out. Regardless of structured or nonstructured, educators must design rituals into the curriculum to help children connect with the community and help them transform into contributing and integrated members of the community. Allen (1992) explains, "Ritual can be defined as a procedure whose purpose is to transform someone or something from one condition or state to another" (p. 80). Western education uses many rituals to help children feel connected to the Western community; attendance, pledge of allegiance, daily schedule, storytime after lunch recess, and sharing are examples. In Indigenous thought, the transformative nature of ritual goes beyond the Western view of ritual; ritual helps children spiritually connect with the rest of the world. Children need to feel integral to the world as though they belong to something, not just dropped onto the world without a sense of place.

Allen (1992) explains, "Ritual-based cultures are founded on the primary assumption that the universe is alive and that it is supernaturally ordered" (p. 80). Using ritual to connect a child with the universe introduces a challenge for Western educators who have been told for years anything religious must be left out of the classroom. Making a spiritual connection with the world may be a difficult message to formulate. Yet children need to feel connected to the world and ritual provides the path. Cajete (1994) says, "Society, rituals, healing ceremonies, sports, pilgrimages, vision quests, and other rites provided the communal context in which individuals might attain one of the Indigenous education's highest goals, that of completing one's self" (p. 179). "But I think it's important to notice that the ritual isn't sacred, it just opens the door to the experience. It isn't only the place that is sacred, we are" (Wheatley, 2002, p. 132). Educators help children develop into complete people by connecting them with their community and the world through the rituals we create. When children feel sacred, they fulfill their journey by developing into whole and contributing humans. Wheatley gives us a glimpse of why children must feel sacred:

> When we don't know that sacred is available in our day-to-day lives, when we have to wait for somebody else to give us the experience, it is very difficult to know ourselves as sacred. In the absence of that knowledge, we more easily accept domination and the loss of our freedom. When sacred becomes a special rather than common experience, it becomes difficult to feel fully alive and fully human. (p. 132)

Dreaming and the visionary foundation

In Indigenous education, an important part of the journey to develop into a whole person comes from dreaming and connecting with the non-concrete world. In Western education, we embrace, in controlled settings, connection with the non-concrete world. Creative writing might be one of those settings. Art might be one of those settings. However, these activities often do not integrate into the education process. Educators tack elements such as art and creative writing into the curriculum and depending on how teachers teach them, these elements may or may not tap into a visionary foundation for children. Western education based on objective reality leaves little room for dreaming. Yet as a culture we seek creative people who see out of the box. These non-linear people can tap into dreams and visions of realities without conforming to the objective reality Western educators believe exist. "Through facilitating the understanding of their dreams and conditioning them for the creative process of visioning, we allow students an avenue for learning that capitalizes on one of the most basic and ancient context for developing self-knowledge" (Cajete, 1994, p. 147).

Do educators feel children will not develop into rational and grounded members of our society if they create fantasylands in their minds? Integral to storytelling, visioning and dreaming help children make sense out of the world. Humans learn from stories, and creating educational contexts encouraging children to dream and envision new realities helps them grasp important educational content. Educators can add strategies to classrooms ensuring children have space to dream and vision. Reflection exercises, journaling, telling stories, art, dance, song, experience with nature, unstructured time, and creative writing integrated throughout the educational experience helps build dreaming and visioning into a child's journey to develop into a complete and contributing person. Other aspects of visioning include a holistic framework and give-and-take complementary relationships with others. By combining these attributes of vision we help children feel connected and develop a sense of purpose and place. As Cajete (1994) says, "Living through vision engenders living for a purpose and, as such, significantly enhances the meaning and quality we find in living" (p. 145).

As the world becomes more complex, we look to children to bring creative solutions to the world and help us out of the global crisis we have created. Educators should help children break out of the artificial boundaries we have created and tap into their deep center of creativity, the world of dreams and visions. A positivist framework would consider this nonsense and suggest we need to focus children's attention on objective reality. The highly creative people in the world who transform the way we interact with the world do everything but adhere to objective reality. Ending a chapter on dialogue with the universe, Senge, Scharmer, Jaworski, and Flowers (2004) summarize what happens to create such profound levels of connectivity and creativity:

> Through genuine engagement within teams or groups, as in Bache's classroom, we discover Sacred Mind "hidden" in plain sight . . . alive within our everyday collective experience. . . . And when we do, we discover as Rosch said, that "action becomes action that supports the whole, that includes everything and does everything that's needed." But of course, the action is not just "our action." It is the by-product of participating more consciously, in dialogue with an unfolding universe. (p. 166)

The tutor and the environmental foundation

We can trace many cases of abuse of power, be they abuses against the environment, children, women, and other cultures to a belief in the separation of humans and the rest of the world (Allen, 1992; Cajete, 1994; Roszak, Gomes, & Kanner, 1995). The principle from Indigenous learning of connection to the rest of the world provides a simple but profound mindset shift. Senge, Smith, Kruschwitz, Laur, and Schley (2008) reference Buckminster Fuller when they describe the need to tend to the whole world saying, "Buckminster Fuller once likened our planet to a spaceship hurtling through the universe. Noting that no instruction book came with 'Spaceship Earth,' he cautioned that if we intend to survive, we need to learn how to look at the planet as one system, as a whole, and steward all its resources accordingly" (p. 179).

Educators providing children with a learning context of connection versus separateness, prevent children from growing up feeling like outsiders. Children learn we all have a purpose and they learn to respect the rest of the world. "Within an indigenous ethical system, nature exists on its own terms, and individual non-humans have their own reasons for existence, independent of human interpretation" (Wildcat & Pierotti, 2000, p. 66). Twice-exceptional children may develop into leaders if educators help them draw from ancient Indigenous ecological wisdom. Cajete in Four Arrows, Cajete, and Lee (2010) says, "If Indigenous wisdom can tell us that it is not just about a more pleasurable experience but something much greater, maybe this deeper ensoulment can help us understand life energy in the world so we can maintain our right relationship to it" (p. 103).

An environmental educational foundation should provide the context for the knowledge children acquire through the educational system. Taking an ecological perspective helps children learn from the world around them. As a tutor, the world around us provides lessons human-generated knowledge cannot. "The Environmental foundation forms a context through which the tribe observed and integrated those understandings, bodies of knowledge, and practices resulting from direct interaction with the natural world" (Cajete, 2005, p. 74). Living systems theory has its origin in the environmental foundation. Important learning comes from a relationship between the organism and its environment in living systems of all kinds. Maturana and Varela (1998) tell us, "Everything we have said points to learning as an expression of structural coupling, which always maintains compatibility between the operation of the organism and its environment" (p. 172).

Many people, not just 2e children, experience a sense of separation and a feeling of lack of place. A growing body of work in ecopsychology (Roszak, Gomes, & Kanner, 1995) explains how this separation from the natural world causes the same phenomenon in adults. Western cultures have made an arbitrary cut between us and nature. "Since the cut between self and natural world is arbitrary, we can make it at the skin, or we can take it as far out as you like – to the deep oceans and distant stars. But the cut is far less important than the recognition of uncertainty about making the cut at all" (Hillman, 1995, p. xix). For children who have different ways of knowing, learning, and experiencing the world, providing them with a sense of connection and a bond to the natural world provides a foundation for their journey to develop into whole and healthy humans. Indigenous learning includes a strong connection with the natural world. In speaking about the ecopsychology of development, Barrows (1995) explains:

> Frances Tustin, the British child analyst, sees the "awareness of bodily separateness" as the tragedy underlying human existence. But bodily separateness, we might argue, is an illusion; my skin is not separate from the air around it, my eyes are not separate from what they see. I would alter Tustin's statement to say that it is indeed the illusion of bodily separateness that is the genuine sorrow, that accounts for our loneliness, that isolates us and leads us to exploit and violate one another, the world we live in, and ultimately, ourselves. (p. 109)

Given the serious nature of the separateness 2e children often feel, educators need to help them connect and feel part of the greater world. These children should have the same opportunity to feel connected that Indigenous children taught in a traditional setting have. Connecting with the natural world gives children a sense of place in history and the world. "Indigenous peoples look around them to get a sense of their place in history, and they depend upon the animals and the plants of their local environments for companionship, as well as for food, clothing, and shelter" (Wildcat & Pierotti, 2000, p. 62). Non-Indigenous people often hold up Indigenous cultures as examples of ecological thought and action and how to connect with the world. Educators must help children learn this connection with Mother Earth from an early age (Allen, 1992; Cajete, 1994; Deloria, & Wildcat, 2001). Roszak (1995) explains ecopsychology and this deep sense of connection with the world as follows:

> Like all forms of psychology, ecopsychology concerns itself with the foundations of human nature and behavior. Unlike other mainstream schools of psychology that limit themselves to the intrapsychic mechanisms or to a narrow social range that may not look beyond the family, ecopsychology proceeds from the assumption that at its deepest level the psyche remains sympathetically bonded to the Earth that mothered us into existence. (p. 5)

Infusing an ecological foundation into the learning of children goes beyond helping them gain a sense of place and connection with the world; it provides them with psychological health, sustaining them through their life's journey. In a complex world, simple solutions to global crises do not help create a sustainable world. We must raise children who inherently understand the connectedness of the world. These children are our future and 2e children who already have different ways of knowing, can lead the way. Simply creating awareness for children early in their education helps the child intuitively see what many adults fail to grasp.

An Indigenous educational framework does not ignore the consequences of human actions. Wildcat and Pierotti (2000) explain, "our Indigenous worldviews and knowledge systems shun the naive dichotomies of Western thought, e.g., material versus spiritual, science versus humanities, and quite predictably the most invidious of Western distinctions – nature versus culture" (p. 63). The ecological views of Indigenous people provide principles based on thousands of years of accumulated experience and knowledge interacting with the world, not primitive and quaint relics of the past (Zimmerman, 2004). "The approaches developed by Indigenous people around the world tax the imagination. Indigenous knowledge bases evolved over thousands of years and hundreds of generations" (Cajete, 1994, p. 79). Bringing a deeper level of understanding to children helps them connect to the world around them and gives them the understanding needed to become vital citizens, confident in the contributions their gifts may offer.

Artistic creation and the artistic foundation

Artistic creation closely aligns with visioning and dreaming. This strategy helps children connect with internal sources of creativity and helps them feel like whole people. "The Artistic foundation contains the practices, mediums, and forms through which we usually express the meanings and understandings we have come to see" (Cajete, 2005, p. 74). Cajete further states, "Art itself becomes a primary source of teaching because it both integrates and documents a profound process of learning" (p. 75). When we have an educational budget crisis in the United States, the first programs to be cut from the curriculum include art, music, and other creative learning (Smith, 1988). "When there are budget pressures, the arts and electives budgets are often the first to be cut" (Senge, 2000, p. 42). These creative electives are cut due to a lack of agreement about the importance of the central nature of these electives to a child's education. We learn from Indigenous education these strategies provide critical learning for children. Smith says, "For many learning-disabled children, academic content – mathematical functions, grammar, syntax, spelling – can be taught and made to stick through the arts" (p. 14). Art as an Indigenous education strategy helps children learn and connect with the world within which they grow up. Art also helps children integrate academic lessons into their learning in a way unavailable in traditional Western education settings. In Four Arrows, Cajete, and Lee (2010), Four Arrows explains the role of art to Indigenous culture:

> In Indigenous ways of thinking, to speak a word, to sing, to paint, to dance, etc., is to initiate a process of vibrational energy that enters into relationships that ultimately connect us back to Nature . . . Art, and I am including music when I say art, to Indigenous cultures in not a form of entertainment, amusement or escape as it often is in dominate cultures. Art represents creations that define place and lead to transformations. (p. 88)

"The creation of art is an alchemy of process in which the artist becomes more himself through each act of true creation" (Cajete, 1994, p. 149). As 2e children have a different way of knowing and seeing the world, participating in art provides an avenue to learn about themselves and connect to the world (Smith, 1988). In Indigenous education, art goes beyond individual expression as an individualistic point of view, it expresses the spiritual and provides for the health of the community. Cajete explains, "The making of art in Indigenous societies provided a pathway to wholeness for both the artist and those who utilized the artist's creations" (p. 158).

The Lab School in Washington, DC provides an example of what Smith discovered; art helps children become whole human beings in a complex world. Art should not be an extra to be added or removed based on budget; it should be a core educational component woven throughout the child's educational experience (Smith, 1988). Smith further explains, "The arts can ignite the whole learning process. To have this effect they need to be central to education, not peripheral" (p. 11). Taking the steps to integrate art into the curriculum, even though as a course it may have been removed, provides a powerful strategy to enhance the learning experience of not only the 2e children but all of the children in the classroom.

As a strategy to help 2e children learn, art helps children connect with the world around them and construct meaning around the rich inputs confronting them. Art helps create concrete connections with the hopes and dreams of children and connects them with the materials they must learn. "Whereas myth is reflective of inner psychology and cultural concepts through imagery and symbol, art gives a concrete and tangible expressive form to these dimensions" (Cajete, 1994, p. 153). As 2e children often have difficulty with words, art helps these children feel they too can communicate. When children grow up, they can inherently represent the world artistically and educators need to tap into this inherent way of knowing the world to ensure children excel on their life learning journeys. As Smith (1988) says, "All art carries symbolic meaning, understood without words. Little children know this. They understand gesture, rhythm, tone, and movement before they understand words" (p. 11).

Part Five
Insights, Conclusions, and Recommendations

"The man who sat on the ground in his tipi meditating on life and its meaning, accepting the kinship of all creatures, and acknowledging unity with the universe of things, was infusing into his being the true essence of civilization."
-- -- Luther Standing Bear,
OGLALA SIOUX

Chapter 17
Insights and Conclusions

When I decided to abandon my Human and Organization Development (HOD) dissertation and pursue an Education Leadership for Change (ELC) dissertation, little did I know the research and writing would create such a profound impact on my life. So many school systems are unresponsive to the needs of 2e children and often the education experience focuses on disabilities and delivery of existing Western knowledge. I have met many people who are 2e or have 2e children and without exception, each is struggling with many of the same problems I experienced in the Western school system. I have learned about myself through the experience of researching and writing this book and have learned about the magnitude of the social injustice in the education system for 2e children. Few school systems seem to be immune to the problems experienced by 2e children. *The Seattle Times* in Seattle, Washington (9/5/2014) spoke of the disarray of special education in the city of Seattle. Six directors in 5 years and angry parents and constituents are attacking the system. Complaints are the norm. The legislature just released a 2-year study conducted by over 300 participants calling for the complete overhaul of not only special education but how we structure all of education in Seattle. The recommendation is to move to a Universal Design for Learning (UDL) approach to education, an approach consistent with my recommendations. I would have thought a city like Seattle would be on top of educating alternative learning children. School systems have a real need for new ideas in this space and this work brings needed innovations to the conversation.

I have brought together seemingly disparate interests to approach reimagining education for 2e children. My research and passion for how humans organize around communication provide the core of my professional work, my research, and my approach to transforming 2e education. Dialogic processes are central to how humans learn, regardless of their age. Through my research in Process Organization Studies (PROS), I see systems in the process of emergence rather than rigid establishments unable to change. New models can emerge through dialogic processes even though it will be difficult to move mindsets within the system. I then bring to my dialogic focus my passion and interest in traditional Indigenous learning. I was drawn to this field because it respected individual learning paths and because of its inherent support for spirit-based and ecologically situated learning with a foundation for systems thinking and multiple pathways. An Indigenous learning approach embraces and engages the whole child helping create fully functioning adults who can and will realize their potentials. Indigenous learning also has an inherent foundation in building on strengths coming from a belief each person is imbued with gifts from the Creator and our job is to recognize and honor those gifts. This ancient learning framework aligns with research in resilience and positive psychology and as well as a large body of work on building on strengths coming from research into employee engagement in organizations.

Although the athletic industry figured out long ago winning requires placing people in roles where they have inherent strengths, in the world of organizations this seems to be new knowledge. Research starting with the groundbreaking book *First Break All the Rules*, Buckingham and Coffman (1999) told the world of organizations to get high performance, they must build on the strengths of their people, not focus on their weaknesses. The research-based on over 80,000 interviews with managers was decisive. Current literature continues to highlight selecting team members on their talent and then developing their strengths. Yet in the world of organization development, too few organization leaders are making this change. This has been frustrating for me as an educator focused on helping leaders shift to this mindset. Education seems to be even further behind the world of business in adopting a strengths-first approach. Indigenous learning principles do exactly this, recognize, honor, and build on the inherent gifts of each child. The pattern of having Indigenous principles far ahead of athletics, then organization development, and then finally education repeats in history. This should not be a surprise as Indigenous principles have been tested and refined over tens of thousands of years. Indigenizing the classroom should be the logical next step for those wanting to develop human capital in communities. Ancient and current leading practices suggest Indigenous principles provide a compelling model for transforming how we teach children.

Indigenizing the classroom also embraces the real complexity found in the world, not just Western views of how the world should work. We can draw from ancient Indigenous wisdom on a variety of fronts to help children learn how to lead in the emerging world. Indigenous principles have not only preceded the Western thinking of building on strengths, but Indigenous principles have also led in democratic governance, matriarchal societies, sustainable communities, systems thinking, bringing multiple generations together in circle and dialogue, and welcoming those with diverse backgrounds into the community. Many who have grown up in Western society have much to learn from ancient Indigenous wisdom. All these Indigenous principles can fit within a cluster grouping approach and are supported by multiple pathways. Nothing about infusing Indigenous learning into the classroom should be revolutionary, but, of course, revolutionary describes the approach well. If only for the fact the Western mindset derives from duality and separateness, and we expect experts to teach us rather than embracing the community and the world around us as sources of learning. Given the prevalent dualistic mindset, Western educators may indeed see this approach as revolutionary. Although educators have a simple solution provided in this book, implementation would not be an easy plug and play as the complexity and emotions around k-12 education will create complications. Western educational systems represent the same complexity, uncertainty, and ambiguity 2e children will experience in the world and which they are uniquely suited to embrace based on their unique combination of gifts and deficits. This very complexity that 2e children thrive in also provides the challenges we face in Indigenizing Western education. Educators see themselves as separate from the very systems they are co-creating. Their mindsets create the dysfunction and social injustice 2e children face day in and day out, they just do not see it. Many 2e children in current and future classrooms will experience similar experiences to my journey, but, of course, each journey will be fundamentally different. I embarked on this research journey to heal myself, help others like me, and influence my community. I also understand the differences in experience while seeing the common thread binding us together on this 2e journey.

I wish I had grown up with Indigenous educational principles as the context for my learning. The greatest impact would have been on my sense of efficacy and my self-esteem from k-5 learning. I believe my life would have been transformed with these principles. My parents provided a loving and stable home and made substantial sacrifices to provide me with the experiences I needed to learn to learn and to read. What was missing was any recognition of my gifts by teachers in my grade school, at least until my fifth through eighth-grade experience at FCDS.

When I introduced this book, I explained I learned differently than others, saw the world differently, and thought differently. The pattern of communicating, thinking, and hard work learned early certainly framed my development and provided the foundation for this research. My worldview also results directly from growing up as a 2e child. While others saw and memorized discrete facts, the

Creator blessed me by seeing connections and patterns. This is born out in the psychological assessment I took before entering my doctoral program at Fielding Graduate University. I intuitively knew I could synthesize disparate inputs into strategic solutions, the language I used to describe my abilities, but not until starting my doctoral journey, which is the foundation for this book, was this made real for me. From my earliest memories, I saw myself connected to the world around me, not separate and disconnected. A holistic worldview has helped me embrace complexity, uncertainty, and ambiguity rather than one-dimensional patterns and solutions. This gift informs my view on topics as diverse as human relations where people co-create their relationships to environmental challenges where simple statements of solution ignore the complexity humans have created. I also understand through the experience of researching and writing my dissertation and this book, the challenges I faced have not only created pain, hardships, setbacks, and patterns of behavior I certainly could have done without, but have also provided me with the gifts of empathy, perseverance in the face of adversity, resilience, a love for creation, and the best gift of all—who I am now. I finally also have clarity about my journey and what being 2e has meant to me. Yes I accept the gifts I have been given, and yes I was blessed with a family who stepped up to help me, but I would like to create a healthier learning environment for other 2e children to improve their chances of realizing their potential. The majority will not have the opportunities I had as I grew up. The world will certainly continue becoming more complex, uncertain, and ambiguous. Twice-exceptional children's gifts must be recognized and nurtured to give them a fighting chance in a very competitive and dynamic world. We need courageous children willing and able to take on these challenges. Indigenous learning principles and Indigenizing classrooms combined with cluster grouping education will help make this happen.

Brendtro and Larson (2004) describe how Nelson Mandela created *The Circle of Courage* "as the basic model of organizing developmental assessment and strength-building interventions" for at-risk youth. The model, in Figure 17.1, was based on the philosophy of helping children develop resilience through developing their strengths. When children can develop their strengths, they thrive. This work is complementary to Indigenous learning principles and can be a model to help in the integration of Indigenous learning principles into Western educational frameworks. The four categories of development in circles of courage include the dimensions of belonging, mastery, independence, and generosity. The authors integrated developmental assets defined by the Search Institute and those from researchers in positive psychology to create a combined model including rich explanations of each dimension. If we set our sights on developing resilient 2e children who are equipped with the confidence to excel with their gifts and the learning tools to help mitigate their deficits, I believe we will have fulfilled our mission.

Educators should not try to take away 2e children's challenges and struggles as we learn best through adversity. Having more children who have been given everything is the last thing we need. But for most 2e children not having enough challenges simply would never happen. These children probably will grow up with and experience plenty of adversities. Educators should help 2e children become whole human beings through guidance and engagement so they can realize their potential. This certainly cannot be asking too much of educators. "All children are endowed with the seed for some unique 'genius.' In the struggle to find their purpose, they make missteps and show many problems. Our task is to provide opportunities so children can discover their destiny and calling" (Brendtro & Larson, 2004, p. 197).

My work on my dissertation and this book helped me discover my destiny and calling. I am glad I listened to my heart to do this work. My initial research into the emerging field of Process

Organization Studies was exciting and compelling as was my research into dialogue and dialogic frameworks. All the research has informed my practice and who I am as a researcher-practitioner. Without my extensive research into these fields of study, I may

Attachment: This growth need is met by opportunities for Belonging.	
Coopersmith:	Significance, acceptance, attention, and affection of others.
Flach:	A network of friends, a community where one is respected, humor.
Werner:	Caring and attentive family environments; if parents are absent or inattentive, extended family, siblings, and other adults provide counsel, safety, and support; participation in school and community programs.
Wolin:	Relationships, humor, intimate and fulfilling ties to others.
Achievement: This growth need is met by opportunities for Mastery.	
Coopersmith:	Competence, success in meeting demands for achievement.
Flach:	Creativity, open-mindedness, receptive to new ideas, wide range of interests, recognizes one's gifts and talents, willing to dream, finds novel solutions to meet goals, redefines assumptions and problems to find solutions.
Werner:	High expectations, academic success, communication skills.
Wolin:	Insight, initiative, creativity, stretches self in demanding tasks, asks tough questions, gives honest answers, brings order and purpose to chaos.
Autonomy: This growth need is met by opportunities for Independence.	
Coopersmith:	Power, the ability to be in charge of self and to be able to influence others.
Flach:	Autonomy, independence of thought and action, personal discipline and responsibility, insight into one's own feelings, high tolerance of distress, distances oneself from destructive relationships.
Werner:	Sense of personal efficacy or control over one's environment.
Wolin:	Independence, keeps boundaries and emotional distance from troubled persons, initiative, takes charge of problems, exerts control.
Altruism: This growth need is met by opportunities for Generosity.	
Coopersmith:	Virtue, adherence to moral and ethical standards.
Flach:	Insight into the feelings of others, hope, commitment, the search for meaning, purpose, faith, a sense of destiny.
Werner:	Empathy and caring, productive roles in family and community life.
Wolin:	Relationships of empathy, capacity to give, morality with an informed conscience, judges right from wrong, values decency, compassion, honesty, fair play, responds to needs and suffering of others.

Figure 17.1 Circle of courage, Brendtro & Larson, 2004.

never have discovered my calling to help children who are growing up as I did, gifted and learning-disabled. The integration and intersection of the many threads of scholarship have truly been compelling. This work not only has helped heal me, I see the possibility to help other 2e children and communities and the opportunity to make meaningful change in the world creating energy I would never have expected. Now, whenever I am asked to talk about my research, my energy level and my excitement escalate. I finally believe in the positive difference I can make in the world by helping 2e children realize their potential through education transformation based on Indigenous learning foundations.

Chapter 18
Future Research Directions and Applications

My research was based on a narrow application of Indigenous learning and cluster-grouped classroom design for gifted and learning-disabled children. This research falls within the Universal Design for Learning (UDL) field of practice. As I am just now implementing this research in a new charter school for immigrant children just outside of Seattle, my hope would be first and foremost to have a co-research practitioner embrace the approach recommended and work with me to research and study its efficacy. I would certainly welcome the opportunity to participate in such a study. As mentioned earlier in the book, a multiplier effect results from the implementation of Indigenous learning within a cluster-grouped classroom. Not only will the gifted and learning-disabled children gain from the framework, but the rest of the children in the clustered grouped classroom will. I would like to see a study that explores the impact on all children in a cluster-grouped classroom based on Indigenous learning. I would like to see if the predicted results of improved learning, self-esteem, and sense of efficacy are validated in all populations of children. An example of a clustered grouped classroom ecosystem is found in Appendix A.

Although not specifically focused on gifted and learning-disabled children, I would like to see the recommendations provided in this book implemented with Indigenous children. Given this vision, a study based solely on an Indigenous school setting would be exciting. We have so much to learn about how to restructure education to improve how we develop all children's gifts; each research project would help get us closer to this goal. I would be interested in seeing educators write specific programs and curricula to integrate Indigenous learning, regardless of whether the application falls within a cluster-grouped classroom. I cannot imagine all the permutations arising from this research, but with that said, I would welcome participating in a broad spectrum of initiatives and conversations to help explore innovations in the application of Indigenous learning in education. All the possible areas for research would be supported by the Universal Design for Learning (UDL) field and reaching out within the UDL community will be a focus as I explore research possibilities.

An intriguing area of research would include how the genetic predisposition for introversion and extroversion impacts the expression of learning exceptionalities. Original work by Harvard's Jerome Kagan and expanded by Dr. Carl Schwartz, the director of the Developmental Neuroimaging and Psychopathology Research Lab at Massachusetts General Hospital and others, provide extraordinary insights into how introversion and extroversion impact how people interact with the world. An introverted 2e child like myself will respond quite differently with his learning environment than an extroverted 2e child. Research into the intersectionality of these two characteristics could prove to be invaluable.

There are two areas of research and application specifically suited to working with Indigenous learning. One such area is systems thinking and teaching children to think systemically. With a deep background in systems thinking research and application, I find systems thinking a natural pairing with Indigenous learning as Indigenous learning at its core supports systems-based thinking. Not only does Indigenous learning integrate systems thinking, but systems thinking also permeates many aspects of Indigenous learning. Peter Senge provided a rich resource for educators and researchers when he wrote the fifth discipline resource guide *Schools That Learn* (Senge et al., 2000). I can see that those school districts that have implemented programs and written curricula to address systems would be open to explore working with Indigenous learning as a systems approach to education. I would like to see these two fields come into conversation and see what emerges at the borderlands between these fields. Linda Booth Sweeney actively works in the field of integration of systems thinking into education. Her book *When a Butterfly Sneezes* (Sweeney, 2001) provides an accessible and engaging approach to teach systems thinking to children using stories. Her work directly addresses two critical Indigenous learning principles—systems thinking and storytelling. I would like to see schools that use her work, also explore using Indigenous learning combined with a research study to publish the results.

The Sustainable Education Every Day (SEED) movement provides another area where Indigenous learning and cluster-grouped classrooms can integrate. SEED initiatives by their very nature are holistic, systems-based, and honor Indigenous learning principles. Seeking learning partners within the SEED movement can provide contexts for studies in Indigenous learning. One such education startup is the SEED Collaborative in Seattle, Washington (www.theSEEDcollaborative.org). This enterprise is building sustainable classrooms designed to provide children with an experiential education within a living classroom. Creating experiences for children to learn from nature, an important component of Indigenous learning, challenges educators in urban or suburban settings and these classrooms can provide children with learning from nature in areas where this might be difficult otherwise. SEED classrooms can directly support Indigenous learning principles of learning from nature, experiential learning, and systems thinking. Schools implementing work in systems and SEED might be more likely to embrace both cluster-grouped classrooms and Indigenous learning and could be important research partners in exploring the transformation of education systems to help children develop their gifts and realize their potential.

Thank you for joining me on this journey. There is so much potential to transform the lives of 2e and other children in our school systems. I hope that this research has provided some new perspectives on how to help our children discover their gifts and fulfill their potential. I would welcome a conversation.

Appendix A

Proposed Classroom For 2e Children

Begin with

Nature inspired classrooms (SEED), access to nature

Select children for cluster-grouped cohorts
- 2e children
- LD children
- Gifted children
- Other exceptionality children
- No exceptionality children

Select teachers who have a passion and talent for cluster-grouped classrooms then train and support them

Develop blended curriculum
- Multiple pathways
- Indigenous learning
- Western knowing
- Systems inspired
- Learner centered
- Experiential

Result

Children knowing gifts and realizing their potential
- Self esteem and efficacy
- Solve complex problems
- Contribute locally/globally
- Systems mentality

Appendix B

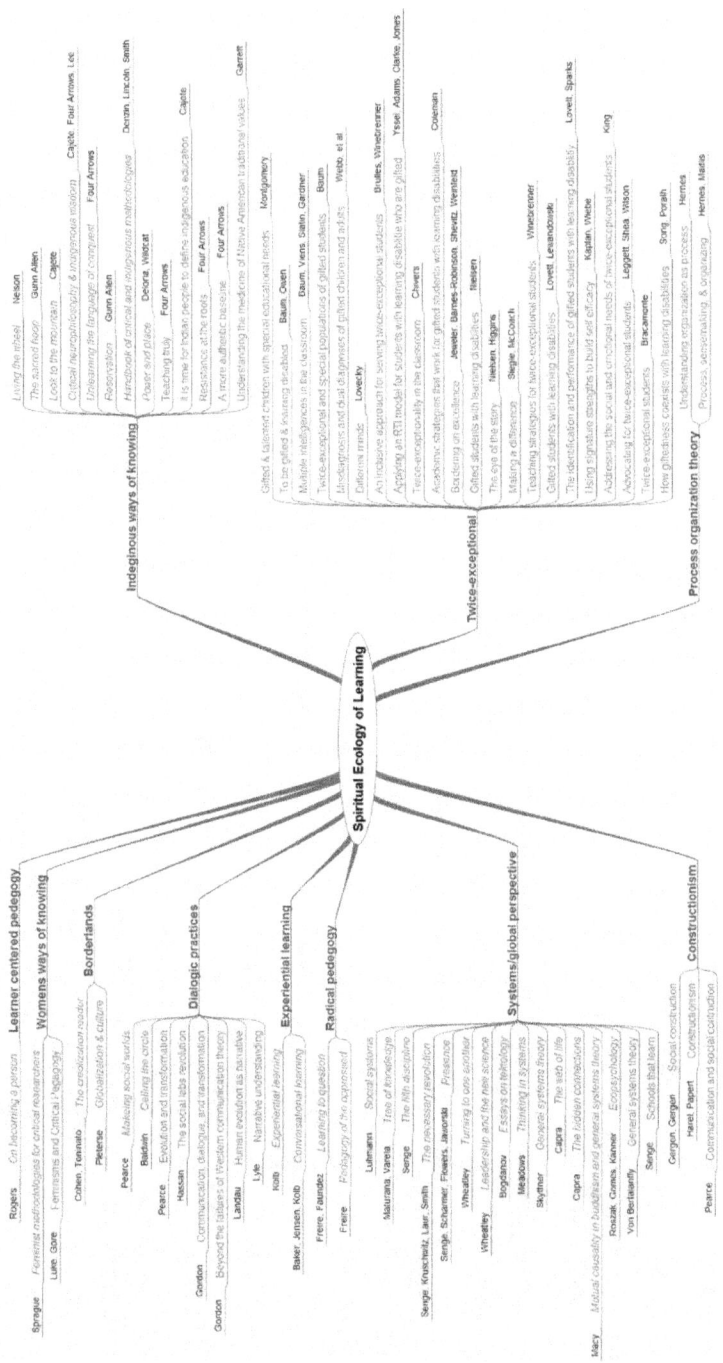

Bibliography

Aboriginal Affairs and Northern Development Canada, Government of Canada. (n.d.). *First Nations*. Retrieved from https://www.aadnc-aandc.gc.ca/eng/1100100013791/1100100013795

Ackermann, E. (2001). Piaget's constructivism, Papert's constructionism: What's the difference? In *Constructivism: Uses and perspectives in education* (pp. 85-94), Volumes 1 & 2. Conference Proceedings. Geneva, Switzerland: Research Center in Education.

Allen, P. G. (1992). *The sacred hoop: Recovering the feminine in American Indian traditions*. Boston, MA: Beacon Press.

Allen, P. G. (1998). *Off the reservation: Reflections on boundary-busting, border-crossing, loose cannons*. Boston, MA: Beacon Press.

American Psychiatric Association. (2013). *Specific learning disorder. DSM-5 Development*. Retrieved from http://www.dsm5.org

Armstrong, J. (1995). Keepers of the earth. In Roszak, T., Gomes, M. E., & Kanner, A. D. (Eds.). *Ecopsychology: Restoring the earth healing the mind* (pp. 316-324). San Francisco, CA: Sierra Club Books.

Assouline, S. G., Foley Nicpon, M., & Huber, D. H. (2006). The impact of vulnerabilities and strengths on the academic experiences of twice-exceptional students: A message to school counselors. *Professional School Counseling*, 10(1), 14-24.

Baker, A. C., Jensen, P. J., & Kolb, D. A. (2002). *Conversational learning: An experiential approach to knowledge creation*. Westport, CT: Quorum Books.

Baldwin, C. (1998). *Calling the circle: The first and future culture.* New York, NY: Bantam Books.

Barrows, A. (1995). The ecopsychology of child development. In T. Roszak, M. E. Gomes, & A. D. Kanner (Eds.), *Ecopsychology: Restoring the earth healing the mind* (pp. 101-110). San Francisco, CA: Sierra Club Books.

Battiste, M. (2008). Research ethics for protecting indigenous knowledge and heritage: Institutional and researcher responsibilities. In N. K. Denzin, Y. S. Lincoln, & L. T. Smith (Eds.), *Handbook of critical and indigenous methodologies* (pp. 497-509). Thousand Oaks, CA: SAGE.

Baum, S. M. (Ed.). (2004). *Twice-exceptional and special populations of gifted students.* Thousand Oaks, CA: Corwin Press.

Baum, S. M. (2012, May 16). What's in a name? Defining and reifying twice-exceptional education. *The 2e Education Blog.* Retrieved from http://twiceexceptional.com/2012/05/16/whats-in-a-name-defining-and-reifying-twice-exceptional-education/#

Baum, S. M., & Owen, S. V. (2004). *To be gifted & learning-disabled: Strategies for helping bright students with LD, ADHD, and more.* Mansfield Center, CT: Creative Learning Press.

Baum, S. M., Viens, J., & Slatin, B. (2005). *Multiple intelligences in the elementary classroom: A teacher's toolkit.* New York, NY: Teachers College Press.

Bogdanov, A. (1980). *Essays on tektology* (George Gorelik, Trans.). Seaside, CA: Intersystems.

Bohm, D. (2008). *On dialogue.* New York, NY: Routledge Classics.

Boyte, H. C. (2009). Civic agency and the cult of the expert: A study for the Kettering Foundation. *Kettering Foundation.*

Bracamonte, M. (2010, March). Twice-exceptional students: Who are they and what do they need? *The 2e Newsletter.* Retrieved from http://www.2enewsletter.com/article_2e_what_are_they.html

Brendtro, L., & Larson, S. (2004). The resilience code: Finding greatness in youth. *Reclaiming Children and Youth, 12*(4), 194-200.

Brulles, D., & Winebrenner, S. (2009, May/June). An inclusive approach for serving twice-exceptional students: The school-wide cluster grouping model. *The 2e Newsletter*, (34).
Brulles, D., & Brown, K. L. (2018). *A Teacher's Guide to Flexible Grouping and Collaborative Learning: Form, Manage, Assess, and Differentiate in Groups*. Minneapolis, MN: Free Spirit Publishing.
Buckingham, M., & Coffman, C. (1999). *First break all the rules: What the world's greatest managers do differently*. New York, NY: Simon & Schuster.
Bushe, G. R. (2009). Dialogic OD: Turning away from diagnosis. In W. Rothwell, R. Sullivan, J. Stravros, & A. Sullivan (Eds.), *Practicing organization development: A guide for managing and leading change* (3rd ed.). San Francisco, CA: Jossey-Bass.
Bushe, G. R., & Marshak, R. J. (2009). Revisioning organization development: Diagnostic and dialogic premises and patterns of practice. *The Journal of Applied Behavioral Science*, 45(3), 378-383.
Cajete, G. (1994). *Look to the mountain: An ecology of indigenous education*. Skyland, NC: Kivaki Press.
Cajete, G. (2005). American Indian epistemologies. *New Directions for Student Services*, 109, 69-78. Retrieved August 14, 2010, from http://www.jbp.com
Cajete, G. (2006). It is time for Indian people to define indigenous education on our own terms. *Tribal College*, 18(2), 56-58. Retrieved August 7, 2010, from http://proquest.umi.com
Campbell, J. (1972). *The hero with a thousand faces*. Princeton, NJ: Princeton University Press.
Capra, F. (1996). *The web of life: The new scientific understanding of living systems*. New York, NY: Anchor Books.
Capra, F. (2002). *The hidden connections: A science for sustainable living*. New York, NY: Anchor Books.
Chang, H. (2007). Autoethnography: Raising cultural consciousness of self and others. In Walford, G. (Ed.), *Methodological developments in ethnography (Studies in Educational Ethnography, Volume 12*, pp.207-221). Bingley, UK: Emerald Group.

Chivers, S. (2012). Twice-exceptionality in the classroom. *Journal of Student Engagement: Education Matters,* 2(1), 26-29.

Clinton, H. (1996). Remarks by First Lady Hillary Rodham Clinton. *The Democratic National Convention in Chicago,* Tuesday, August 27, 1996. Retrieved August 15, 2010 from http://www.happinessonline.org/LoveAndHelpChildren/p12.htm

Cohen, R., & Toninato, P. (2010). Introduction: The creolization debate: Analysing mixed identities and cultures. In R. Cohen, & P. Toninato (Eds.), *The creolization reader: Studies in mixed identities and cultures* (pp. 1-21). New York, NY: Routledge.

Coleman, M. R. (2005). Academic strategies that work for gifted students with learning disabilities. *Teaching Exceptional Children,* 38(1), 28-32.

Deloria, V., & Wildcat, D. R. (2001). *Power and place: Indian education in America.* Golden, CO: Fulcrum.

Doidge, N. (2007). *The brain that changes itself: Stories of personal triumph from the frontiers of brain science.* New York, NY: Penguin Books.

Egan, K. (1991). *Primary understanding: Education in early childhood.* New York, NY: Routledge.

Egan, K. (1992). *Imagination in teaching and learning ages 8-15.* London, UK: Routledge.

Ellis, C., Adams, T., & Bochner, A. (2010). Autoethnography: An overview. *Forum Qualitative Sozialforschung / Forum: Qualitative Social Research,* 12(1). Retrieved from http://www.qualitative-research.net/index.php/fqs/article/view/1589/3095

Four Arrows (2013). *Teaching truly: A curriculum to Indigenize mainstream education.* New York, NY: Peter Lang.

Four Arrows (2014). Resistance at the roots: Indigenizing mainstream education to end neoliberal violence. In M. Abendroth, & B. J. Portilio (Eds.), *School against neoliberal rule: Educational fronts for local and global justice: A reader.* Charlotte, NC: Information Age.

Four Arrows, Cajete, G., & Lee, J. (2010). *Critical neurophilosophy & Indigenous wisdom.* Rotterdam, The Netherlands: Sense.

Four Arrows, & Narvaez, D. (2015) Reclaiming our Indigenous worldview: A more authentic baseline for Social/ecological justice work in education. In N.E. McCrary, & E.W. Ross (Eds.) *Working for social justice inside and outside the classroom: A community of students, teachers, researchers and activists* (pp. 93-112). New York, NY: Peter Lang.

Freire, P. (2009). *Pedagogy of the oppressed* (30th Anniversary edition). New York, NY: Continuum.

Freire, P., & Faundez, A. (1989). *Learning to question: A pedagogy of liberation* (T. Coates, Trans.). New York, NY: Crossroad/Continuum.

Freire, P., & Macedo, D. (1995). A dialogue: Culture, language, and race. *Harvard Educational Review,* 65(3), 377-402. Retrieved September 4, 2010, from Research Library Core. (Document ID: 6755799).

Garrett, M. T., (1999). Understanding the "medicine" of Native American traditional values: An integrative review. *Counseling and Values,* 43(2), 84-98.

Gergen, K. J., & Gergen, M. M. (2004). *Social construction: Entering the dialogue.* Chagrin Falls, OH: Taos Institute.

Gergen, M., & Gergen, K. (2002). Ethnographic representation as relationship. In A. Bochner, & C. Ellis (Eds.), *Ethnographically speaking: Autoethnography, literature, and aesthetics* (pp. 11-33). Walnut Creek, CA: Altamira.

Gordon, R. D. (2006). Communication, dialogue, and transformation. *Human Communication: Journal of the Asian & Pacific Communication Association,* 9, 17-30.

Gordon, R. D. (2007). Beyond the failures of Western communication theory. *Journal of Multicultural Discourses,* 2(2), 89-107. Retrieved August 7, 2010, from http://web.ebscohost.com.ezproxy.fielding.edu

Harel, I. E., & Papert, S. E. (1991). *Constructionism.* Norwood, NJ: Ablex.

Hassan, Z. (2014). *The social labs revolution: A new approach to solving our most complex challenges*. San Francisco, CA: Berrett-Koehler.

Hernes, T. (2008). *Understanding organization as process: Theory for a tangled world*. New York, NY: Routledge.

Hernes, T. (2010). Actor-network theory, Callon's Scallops, and process-based organization studies. In T. Hernes, & S. Maitlis (Eds.), *Process, sensemaking, & organizing* (pp. 161-184). New York, NY: Oxford University Press.

Hernes, T., & Maitlis, S. (Eds.). (2010). *Process, sensemaking, & organizing*. New York, NY: Oxford University Press.

Hillman, J. (1995). A psyche the size of earth: A psychological forward. In T. Roszak, M. E. Gomes, & A. D. Kanner (Eds.), *Ecopsychology: Restoring the earth healing the mind* (pp. xvii-xxiii). San Francisco, CA: Sierra Club Books.

Inman, J., & Thompson, T. A. (2013). Using dialogue then deliberation to transform a warring leadership team. *Organization Development Practitioner, 45*(1), 35-40.

International Work Group for Indigenous Affairs. (n.d.). *Indigenous peoples in Latin American – a general overview*. Retrieved from http://www.iwgia.org/regions/latin-america/indigenous-peoples-in-latin-america

Jeweler, S., Barnes-Robinson, L., Shevitz, B. R., & Weinfeld, R. (2008). Bordering on excellence: A teaching tool for twice-exceptional students. *Gifted Child Today*, 31(2), 40-46.

Kaplan, A., & Wiebe, C. (2013, March). Using signature strengths to build self efficacy: Positive psychology and the 2e learner. *The 2e Newsletter*. Retrieved from http://www.2enewsletter.com/subscribers_only/arch_2013_03_Positive_Psych_&_2e_Learner.html

Kincheloe, J. L., & Steinberg, S. R. (2008). Indigenous knowledges in education: Complexities, dangers, and profound benefits. In N. K. Denzin, Y. S. Lincoln, & L. T. Smith (Eds.), *Handbook of critical and indigenous methodologies* (pp. 135-156). Thousand Oaks, CA: SAGE.

King, E. W. (2005). Addressing the social and emotional needs of twice-exceptional students. *Teaching Exceptional Children*, 38(1), 16-20.

Kolb, D. A. (1984). *Experiential learning: Experience as the source of learning and development.* Englewood Cliffs, NJ: Prentice-Hall.

Lakoff, G., & Johnson, M. (1980). *Metaphors we live by.* Chicago, IL: Chicago University Press.

Landau, M. (1984). Human evolution as narrative. *American Scientist*, 72, 262-268. Retrieved August 20, 2010, from http://www.stanford.edu

Leggett, D. G., Shea I., & Wilson, J. A. (2010). Advocating for twice-exceptional students: An ethical obligation. *Research in Schools*, 17(2), 1-10.

Lessem, R., & Schieffer, A. (2008). *Integral research: A global approach towards social science research leading to social innovation.* Geneva, Switzerland: TRANS4M.

Lovecky, D. V. (2004). *Different minds: Gifted children with AD/HD, Asperger Syndrome, and other learning deficits.* Philadelphia, PA: Jessica Kingsley.

Lovett, B. J., & Lewandowski, L. J. (2006). Gifted students with learning disabilities: Who are they? *Journal of Learning Disabilities*, 39(6), 515-527.

Lovett, B. J., & Sparks, R. L. (2011). The identification and performance of gifted students with learning disability diagnoses: A quantitative synthesis. *Journal of Learning Disabilities*, 46(4), 304-316.

Luhmann, N. (1995). *Social systems.* Stanford, CA: Stanford University Press.

Luke, C., & Gore, J. (Eds.). (1992). *Feminisms and critical pedagogy.* New York, NY: Routledge.

Lyle, S. (2000). Narrative understanding: Developing a theoretical context for understanding how children make meaning in classroom settings. *Journal of Curriculum Studies*, 32(1), 45-63. Retrieved August 21, 2010, from http://dx.doi.org/10.1080/002202700182844

Macdonald, S. J. (2009). Windows of reflection: Conceptualizing dyslexia using the social model of disability. *Dyslexia*, 15, 347-362. Retrieved August 14, 2010, from http://www.interscience.wiley.com

Macy, J. (1991). *Mutual causality in Buddhism and general systems theory: The dharma of natural systems*. New York: State University of New York Press.

Mann, T. (1960). Freud and the future. In H. A. Murray (Ed.), *Myth and mythmakers* (p. 374). New York, NY: George Braziller.

Marshak, R. J. (2009). *Organizational change: Views from the edge*. Bethel, ME: The Lewin Center.

Marshak, R. J., & Bushe, G. R. (2009). Further reflections on diagnostic and dialogic forms of organization development. *The Journal of Applied Behavioral Science*, 45, 348-368.

Marshak, R. J., & Grant, D. (2011). Creating change by changing the conversation. *OD Practitioner*, 43, 2-7.

Maturana, H., & Varela, F. (1998). *The tree of knowledge: The biological roots of human understanding* (rev. ed.). Boston, MA: Shambhala.

Meadows, D.H. (2008). *Thinking in systems: A primer*. White River Junction, VT: Chelsea Green.

Montgomery, D. (2003). *Gifted & talented children with special educational needs: Double exceptionality*. New York, NY: Routledge.

National Congress of American Indians. (n.d.). *An introduction to Indian nations in the United States*. Retrieved from http://www.ncai.org/about-tribes/indians_101.pdf

Neihardt, J. G. (1988). *Black Elk speaks: Being the life story of a holy man of the Oglala Sioux*. Lincoln: University of Nebraska Press.

Nelson, A. (1993). *Living the wheel: Working with emotion, terror, and bliss through imagery*. York Beach, ME: Samuel Weiser.

Nielsen, M. E. (2002). Gifted students with learning disabilities: Recommendations for identification and programming. *Exceptionality: A Special Education Journal*, 10(2), 93-111. Retrieved 01 December, 2013 from http://dx.doi.org/10.1207/S15327035EX1002_4

Nielsen, M. E., & Higgins, L. D. (2005). The eye of the story: Services and programs for twice-exceptional learners. *Teaching Exceptional Children*, 38(1), 8-15.

Palmer, P. J. (1998). *The courage to teach: Exploring the inner landscape of a teacher's life.* San Francisco, CA: Jossey – Bass.

Pearce, W. B. (2007). *Making social worlds: A communication perspective.* Malden, MA: Blackwell.

Pearce, W. B. (2009a). Communication and social construction: claiming our birthright. In W. Leeds-Hurwitz, & G. Galanes (Eds.), *Socially Constructing Communication* (pp. 33-56). Cresskill, NJ: Hampton Press.

Pearce, W. B. (2009b). Evolution and transformation: A brief history of CMM and a meditation on what using it does to us. In C. Creede, B. Fisher-Yoshida, & P.V. Gallegos (Eds.), *The reflective, facilitative, and interpretive practices of the Coordinated Management of Meaning* (pp. 1-22). Lanham, MD: Rowman & Littlefield.

Pieterse, J. N. (2009). *Globalization & culture: Global melange.* New York, NY: Rowman & Littlefield.

Ricoeur, P. (2010). Being a stranger. *Theory, Culture & Society*, 27(5), 37-48.

Rogers, C. R. (1995). *On becoming a person.* Boston, MA: Houghton Mifflin.

Roszak, T. (1995). Where psyche meets Gaia. In T. Roszak, M. E. Gomes, & A. D. Kanner (Eds.), *Ecopsychology: Restoring the earth healing the mind* (pp. 1-17). San Francisco, CA: Sierra Club Books.

Roszak, T., Gomes, M. E., & Kanner, A. D. (Eds.). (1995). *Ecopsychology: Restoring the earth healing the mind.* San Francisco, CA: Sierra Club Books.

Senge, P. (2000). The industrial age system of education. In P. Senge, N. Cambron-McCabe, T. Lucas, B. Smith, J. Dutton, & A. Kleiner, *Schools that learn: A fifth discipline fieldbook for educators, parents, and everyone who cares about education* (pp. 27-58). New York, NY: Doubleday.

Senge, P., Cambron-McCabe, N., Lucas, T., Smith, B., Dutton, J., & Kleiner, A. (2000). *Schools that learn: A fifth discipline fieldbook for educators, parents, and everyone who cares about education*. New York, NY: Doubleday.

Senge, P., Scharmer, C. O., Jaworski, J., & Flowers, B. S. (2004). *Presence: Human purpose and the field of the future.* Cambridge, MA: The Society for Organizational Learning.

Senge, P., Smith, B., Kruschwitz, N., Laur, J., & Schley, S. (2008). *The necessary revolution: How individuals and organizations are working together to create a sustainable world.* New York, NY: Doubleday.

Senge, P. M. (1990). *The fifth discipline: The art & practice of the learning organization.* New York, NY: Doubleday/Currency.

Siegle, D., & McCoach, D. B. (2005). Making a difference: Motivating gifted students who are not achieving. *Teaching Exceptional Children, 38*(1), 22-27.

Skyttner, L. (2008). *General systems theory: Problems, perspectives, practice* (2nd ed.). Hackensack, NJ: World Scientific.

Smith, S. L. (1988). The role of the arts in the education of learning-disabled children. *The Pointer, 32*(3), 11-16. Retrieved September 1, 2010, from https://ill.lib.umich.edu/

Song, K., & Porath, M. (2011). How giftedness coexists with learning disabilities: Understanding gifted students with learning disabilities (GLD) in an integrated model of human abilities. *Talent Development & Excellence, 3*(2), 215-227.

Sorensen, M. (2013). The STAR Navajo school model. In Four Arrows, *Teaching truly: A curriculum to Indigenize mainstream education.* (pp. 51-63) New York, NY: Peter Lang.

Sprague, J. (2005). *Feminist methodologies for critical researchers: Bridging differences.* Walnut Creek, CA: AltaMira Press.

Subotnik, R. F., Olszewski-Kubilius, P., & Worrell, F. C. (2011). Rethinking giftedness and gifted education: A proposed direction forward based on psychological science. *Psychological Science in the Public Interest, 12*(1), 3-54.

Sweeney, L. B. (2001). *When a butterfly sneezes: A guide for helping kids explore interconnections in our world through favorite stories.* Waltham, MA: Pegasus Communications.

Taylor, J. R., & Van Every, E. J. (2008). *The emergent organization: Communication as its site and surface.* New York, NY: Psychology Press.

U.S. Department of Education, Office of Special Education Programs, 2008, & 2013. *Statistics of public elementary and secondary school systems,* Washington, DC: National Center for Education Statistics. Retrieved from http://nces.ed.gov/

Von Bertalanffy, L. (1969). *General system theory: Foundations, development, applications* (rev. ed.). New York, NY: George Braziller.

Webb, J. T., Amend, E. R., Webb, N. E., Goerss, J., Beljan, P., & Olenchak, F. R. (2005). *Misdiagnosis and dual diagnoses of gifted children and adults.* Scottsdale, AZ: Great Potential Press.

Wheatley, M.J. (1999). *Leadership and the new science: Discovering order in a chaotic world.* San Francisco, CA: Berrett-Koehler.

Wheatley, M.J. (2002). *Turning to one another: Simple conversations to restore hope to the future.* San Francisco, CA: Berrett-Koehler.

Whitinui, P. (2013). Indigenous autoethnography: Exploring, engaging, and experiencing "self" as a Native method of inquiry. *Journal of Contemporary Ethnography, 43*(4), 456-487. Retrieved July 12, 2014, from http://jce.sagepub.com/content/43/4/456

Wildcat, D. (2001). Indigenizing education: Playing to our strengths. In V. Deloria, & D. Wildcat, *Power and place: Indian education in America.* Golden, CO: Fulcrum.

Wildcat, D., & Pierotti, R. (2000). Finding the indigenous in indigenous studies. *Indigenous Nations Studies Journal, 1*(1), 61-70. Retrieved August 30, 2010, from http://www.eric.ed.gov/

Winebrenner, S. (2003). Teaching strategies for twice-exceptional students. *Intervention in School and Clinic, 38*(3), 131-137.

Winebrenner, S., & Brulles, D. (2008). *The cluster grouping handbook: How to challenge gifted students and improve achievement for all.* Minneapolis, MN: Free Spirit.

Yssel, N., Adams, C., Clarke, L. S., & Jones, R. (2014). Applying an RTI model for students with learning disabilities who are gifted. *Teaching Exceptional Children, 46*(3), 42-52.

Zimmerman, M. J. (2004). Being nature's mind: Indigenous ways of knowing and planetary consciousness. *ReVision*, March 22, 2004. Retrieved June 13, 2014 http://www.highbeam.com/doc/1G1-119071534.html

Index

Page numbers followed by *f*, indicate figures.

2e. *See* twice-exceptional children

Adams, Cheryll, 106, 115–116
adult education degree, 75
affective foundations, 126, 141
Allen, Paula Gunn, 142, 151, 152–153
alphabet children, 110*f*, 111
Alphabetic-Phonic-Syllabic-Linguistic (APSL) programs, 109
alternative learning children, 21–24, 26–29, 46–47, 85, 105–107, 112–113, 165
American Psychological Association, 10–11
animals, working with, 70
Arkansas, summer in, 41–44
art, in education, 130, 154
artistic foundations, 127, 141, 159–161
assessments, of learning disabilities, 88–89
autoethnographic approach, xvii–xxiv, xx*f*

Baker, Ann C., 147
Barnes-Robinson, Linda, 117, 129
Barrows, Anita, 157
Baum, Susan, 7–8, 98, 104, 111–113

Bogdanov, Alexandr, 138
Bohm, David, 146
borderlands, 24–26, 28, 81, 93
Boyte, Harry, 136
Bracamonte, Micaela, 119–120
Brain Fitness Program, The, 87
Brain That Changes Itself, The, 87
Brendtro, Larry, 15, 170–171
Brulles, Dina, 115–116
Buckingham, Marcus, 166

Cajete, Gregory
   on the affective, 152
   on art in education, 130–131
   on artistic foundations, 159–160
   on ecology and education, 140–143
   on holistic education, 136–138
   on Indigenous ecological wisdom, 156
   on Indigenous learning principles, 123–128
   on myths, 150
   on rituals, 153
   on storytelling, 149
   on visionary foundations, 155
Chivers, Stephanie, 116
Circle of Courage, 170–171
circles, spiritual ecology and, 125, 143, 145
Clarke, Laura S., 106, 115–116

classrooms. *See* cluster-grouped classrooms
Clinton, Hillary, 148
cluster-grouped classrooms, 85, 97–98, 106–107, 115–116, 173–175
Coffman, Curt, 166
Coleman, Mary Ruth, 116
collaborative learning. *See* experiential learning
communal foundations, 125, 141
communication, transmission model of, 93
consulting business, 77
conversational learning. *See* experiential learning
coordinated management of meaning (CMM), 93
creative writing, 154
Crittenden, Abe and Eve, 56, 59
culture, 91–92

Developmental Neuroimaging and Psychopathology Research Lab (Massachusetts General Hospital), 174
Dewey, John, 17
Diagnostic and Statistical Manual of Mental Disorders (DSM-5), 11, 23
dialogue
    2e learning and, 27–28
    external barriers to, 91–95
    internal barriers to, 86–91
    sense of community and, 146
dialogue then deliberation model, 93*f*
Different minds: Gifted children with AD/HD, Asperger Syndrome, and other learning deficits (Lovecky), 114
dreaming, 154–155
DSM-5. *See* Diagnostic and Statistical Manual of Mental Disorders (DSM-5)
dual exceptionality. *See* twice-exceptional children
dualistic approach, 92, 94, 128–129, 142–143. *See also* borderlands; Western worldview
dysgraphia, 44
dyslexia, 37

ecopsychology, 157–159
education. *See also* Indigenous learning principles; twice-exceptional children
    dreaming and, 154–155
    holistic, 142
    Indigenizing, 15–19, 92–94, 98, 107–109, 113–115, 141–142, 167–169
    multiple pathways of, 144*f*
    rituals and, 152–153
    strengths of children and, 119
    tips for teachers, 117–118
    Western, 22–23, 105, 128–131, 136–139, 145–154, 165–171
Egan, Kieran, 149, 151
environmental foundations, 127, 141, 155–159
epistemology, 138
experiential learning, 140–141, 145–149, 174
extroversion vs. introversion, 174

Fielding Graduate University, 4
First Break All the Rules (Buckingham and Coffman), 166–172
Flowers, Betty Sue, 155
Ford Country Day School (FCDS), 50–53, 50*f*, 55–56
Four Arrows
    on Indigenizing mainstream education, 15–16, 123–124, 128–130
    on the role of art, 160
    on worldviews, 103
Freire, Paulo, 147–149

gifted and learning-disabled children. *See* twice-exceptional children
gifted and learning-disabled patterns, 9f
Gifted and Talented Children with Special Educational Needs: Double Exceptionality (Montgomery), 107–109
giftedness, 12, 21–22
Gordon, Ronald D., 138

Hassan, Zaid, 23
Higgins, L. Dennis, 117
high schools, culture of, 68
holistic frameworks, 136–140

Indigenous Education, dimensions of, 126f
Indigenous learning principles
    2e learning and, 16–17, 21–29, 103–104, 106–107, 125–131
    advantages of, 166–175
    the arts and, 159–161
    call to action for, 98
    in the classroom, 116–121
    ecology and, 141–145
    High School Years and, 64–67
    living system approach of, 137–140
    Middle School Years and, 51–56
    natural world and, 157
    Pecos River Learning Centers and, 78–80
    project-based learning and, 76–77
    storytelling and, 149–152
    use of, 4–5
    Western education and, 72
    worldview and, 135–140
Indigenous vs. Western living, 25f
Indigenous worldview, 4, 16, 22–23, 26–28, 103, 131. *See also* Indigenous learning principles; Western worldview; worldviews
Inman, John
    eighth-grade graduating class, 53f
    family of, 33–35
    high school experiences, 61–68
    IQ chart of, 10f
    K-5 experiences, 37–47
    with Larry Wilson, 80f
    middle school experiences, 51–60
    note home, 43f
    with puppy, 71f
    at radio station, 78f
Inman, Louis Howard, 67f
introversion vs. extroversion, 174
IQ and performance, 8–10
Irlen reading glasses, 90
Irlen Syndrome, 90

Jaworski, Joseph, 155
Jensen, Patricia J., 147
Jeweler, Sue, 117, 129
Joint Commission of Twice-Exceptional Education, 7
Jones, Ruth, 106, 115–116
Jordan Junior High School, 63

Kaplan, Adam, 119
King, Emily W., 119
Kolb, David A., 147
Kruschwitz, Nina, 156

languages, 103
Larson, Scott, 15, 170–171
Laur, Joe, 156
learning deficits, 10–11
learning environments, 4
learning-disabled children, 3, 7, 86–89, 111–113, 172. *See also* twice-exceptional children
Lee, Jongmin, 143, 156

196 Index

Leggett, Debra G., 115, 120
Lewandowski, Lawrence J., 120
Look to the Mountain (Cajete), 125–128
Lovecky, Deirdre V., 114
Lovett, Benjamin J., 22, 118, 120
Luhmann, Niklas, 138
Lyle, Sue, 146, 151
Lytton School, 38*f*, 40*f*

Macdonald, Stephen J., 137
Macedo, Donaldo, 148
Mansfield, Arkansas, 41*f*, 42*f*
Maturana, Humberto R., 156
McCoach, D. Betsy, 117
Meadows, Donella H., 140
mechanistic systems, 136–138
Misdiagnosis and dual diagnoses of gifted children and adults (Webb et al.), 113
Montgomery, Diane, 27, 107, 113
Multiple Intelligences in the Classroom: A Teacher's Toolkit (Baum, Viens, and Slatin), 112–113
mythic foundations, 125, 141
myths. *See* storytelling

Narvaez, Darcia, 103
National Association for Gifted Children, 113
Neihardt, John G., 145
Nelson, Annabelle, 151
Nielsen, M. Elizabeth, 117
Nishimachi International School, 61–63, 62*f*

objectivist approach, 146
Olszewski-Kubilius, Paula, 12
Oregon State University, 69, 75–76
organizational development, 92
Owen, Steven, 111–112
Palmer, Parker J., 18, 139

Palo Alto High School, 64
Pearce, W. Barnett, 93, 152
Pecos River Learning Centers, 79–80
Pierotti, Raymond, 158
Plantation farm camp, 56–59
Porath, Marion, 120–121
positivism, 136, 139–140, 142, 148, 151, 155
Process Organization Studies (PROS), 94, 103–104, 166
project-based learning, 76–77

religion vs. spiritual ecology, 145
response to intervention (RTI), 106, 116
rituals, 152–153
Rogers, Carl R., 147
Roszak, Theodore, 158

Scharmer, C. Otto, 155
Schley, Sara, 156
School Mathematics Study Group (SMSG), 39
schools, public vs. private, 52, 105
Schools That Learn (Senge), 174–175
school-wide cluster grouping model (SCGM), 106–107, 116. *See also* cluster-grouped classrooms
Scotopic Sensitivity Syndrome, 89–90
Seattle Times, 165
Senge, Peter, 135, 137, 155–156, 174
seven-direction model, 141
Shea, Irene, 115, 120
Shevitz, Betty Roffman, 117, 129
Siegle, Del, 117
Slatin, Barbara, 98, 104
Smith, Bryan, 156
Smith, Sally L., 159–161
social injustice, 46, 56, 97, 99, 124, 168
Song, Kwang-Hoon, 120–121
Sorensen, Mark, 19

Sparks, Richard L., 22, 118
spiritual ecology, 56, 93, 125, 141, 142–145, 144f
STAR Navajo School, 19
storytelling, 149–152
Subotnik, Rena, 12
Sustainable Education Every Day (SEED), 175
Sweeney, Linda Booth, 175
systems thinking, 138–139, 166–167, 173–174

Taylor, James R., 28
teachers, tips for, 117–118
Teaching Truly: A Curriculum to Indigenize Mainstream Education (Four Arrows), 128–131
To Be Gifted & Learning-disabled: Strategies for Helping Bright Students with LD, ADHD, and More (Baum and Owen), 111
transmission model of communication, 93
Twice-exceptional and special populations of gifted students (Baum), 113
twice-exceptional children
 characteristics of, 112
 education of, 15–19, 22–24, 108–121, 165–172
 experience of, 3, 21, 29, 35–36, 70–73, 78, 90–91
 needs of, 8
 signature strengths of, 119
 statistics of, 21–22
 tests for, 118–119
twice-exceptional experiences, 81–84
twice-exceptional learning, literature review, 107–121

undergraduate experiences, 69–73

Universal Design for Learning (UDL), 27, 165, 173–174
U.S, Department of Education, 21

Van Every, Elizabeth J., 28
Varela, Francisco J., 156
Viens, Julie, 98, 104
visionary foundations, 127, 141, 154–155
Von Bertalanffy, Ludwig, 138

Warner, Brent, 50–52, 55, 59
Webb, James T., 114
Wechsler Adult Intelligence Scale, 9–10
Weinfeld, Rich, 117, 129
Western vs. Indigenous living, 25f
Western worldview, 3–4, 22–28, 103, 131, 136, 167. *See also* education; Indigenous worldview; worldviews
Wheatley, Margaret J., 153
When a Butterfly Sneezes (Sweeney), 175
Wiebe, Chris, 119
Wildcat, Daniel, 158
Wilson, Joseph A., 115
Wilson, Larry, 79–81, 80f, 120
Winebrenner, Susan, 115–116, 117
Woodcock-Johnson III Test of Achievement, 9–10
worldviews. *See also* Indigenous worldview; Western worldview
 borderlands and, 24, 26, 56, 78, 81, 95
 co-creation of, 26, 28, 86, 93
 development by children, 137
 holistic, 3, 23, 135, 139, 169
Worrell, Frank, 12

Yssel, Nina, 106, 115–116

About the Author

Dr. Inman has been blessed with both gifted and deficit exceptionalities. He grew up believing he was broken and in need of fixing, a frame of mind that has haunted him his whole life. He did not realize he had gifts until conducting research for his doctorate in education. Rather than just experience the impact of being 2e, Dr. Inman decided to do something about the experience other children have growing up feeling broken and in need of fixing. This book is the outcome of that mission.

With extensive experience and a deep understanding of how humans organize into communities, communicate through dialogue to create meaningful and lasting change, and how humans of all ages learn, grow and contribute to the world, he helps educators collaborate to craft unique paths forward to transform how children and adults learn together.

Dr. Inman grew up unable to read the way his school system taught and understands how so many children wither in the predominant education systems. His work is founded on the concept of Universal Design for Learning (UDL) and any strategy that helps move a school system toward teaching the way children learn vs. forcing children to learn how the teacher teaches is of interest. Dr. Inman embraces learning strategies that include traditional Indigenous learning, andragogy, flipped classrooms, cognitive processes design, green inspired classrooms (SEED), multiple pathways, systems thinking, cluster-grouped classrooms, technology-assisted learning, situated learning, and scenario-based learning. He helps education communities design their transformation approach based on these and any number of other strategies.

Dr. Inman earned his doctorate in educational leadership for change from Fielding Graduate University in 2015 and currently is the founding faculty for the applied management bachelors' program at Tacoma Community College in Tacoma Washington.

Contact Dr. Inman at john@learningexceptionalities.com to explore how he might support the transformation of your educational community or visit him on his web site at www.learningexceptionalities.com.

www.ingramcontent.com/pod-product-compliance
Lightning Source LLC
Chambersburg PA
CBHW071232080526
44587CB00013BA/1582